LAND WARFARE
Brassey's New Battlefield Weapons Systems Series and Technology
into the 21st Century

Volume 3

●●●●●●●●

GUNS, MORTARS AND ROCKETS

LAND WARFARE
Brassey's New Battlefield Weapons Systems and Technology Series
into the 21st Century

Editor-in-Chief: Colonel R G Lee OBE, Former Military Director of Studies,
Royal Military College of Science, Shrivenham,
UK.

The success of the first and second series on Battlefield Weapons Systems and Technology and the pace of advances in military technology have prompted Brassey's to produce a new Land Warfare Series. This series updates subjects covered in the original series and also covers completely new areas. The new books are written for military personnel who wish to advance their professional knowledge. In addition, they are intended to aid anyone who is interested in the design, development and production of military equipment.

0200 049919 124239 002

GUNS, MORTARS AND ROCKETS

• • • • • • • •

M P Manson

Royal Military College of Science, Shrivenham, UK

BRASSEY'S

London · Washington

Copyright © 1997 Brassey's (UK) Ltd

First English Edition 1982
Revised Edition 1997

UK editorial offices: Brassey's, 33 John Street, London, WC1N 2AT
UK orders: Marston Book Services, PO Box 269, Abingdon, OX14 4SD

North American orders: Brassey's Inc., PO Box 960,
Herndon, VA 22070, USA

M P Manson has asserted his moral right to be identified as
the author of this work.

Library of Congress Cataloging in Publication Data
available

British Library Cataloguing in Publication Data

A catalogue record for this book is available from the British Library

ISBN 1 85753 172 8 hardcover

Any views expressed are those of the author and do not necessarily represent the views of the
Department/HM Government.

The front cover shows an AS90 firing (photo by courtesy of DTEO Eskmeals/ Crown Copyright)

The title pages show an AS90 Self-Propelled Howitzer (photo by courtesy of DTEO Eskmeals/
Crown Copyright)

Typeset by Pantek Arts, Maidstone, Kent
Printed in Great Britain by Redwood Books, Trowbridge

Preface

THE SERIES

This series of books is written for those who wish to improve their knowledge of military weapons and equipment. It is equally relevant to professional soldiers, those involved in developing or producing military weapons or indeed anyone interested in the art of modern warfare.

All the texts are written in a way which assumes no mathematical knowledge and no more technical depth than would be gleaned from school days. It is intended that the books should be of particular interest to army officers who are studying for promotion examinations, furthering their knowledge at specialist arms schools or attending command and staff schools.

The authors of the books are all members of the staff of the Royal Military College of Science, Shrivenham, which is comprised of a unique blend of academic and military experts. They are not only leaders in the technology of their subjects, but are aware of what the military practitioner needs to know. It is difficult to imagine any group of persons more fitted to write about the application of technology to the battlefield.

VOLUME III

This is a completely updated and largely rewritten version of the original volume of the same title, first published in 1982. It begins with a brief review of the historical development of artillery, emphasising the interdependence between doctrine and technology which is still a fundamental factor in weapons design today. The indirect fire system is then examined in order to demonstrate the need for a systems approach to current and future developments. The three types of weapon launchers – mortars, guns and rockets – and their associated munitions are then compared in terms of their general characteristics, after which each is considered in detail. The final chapter looks to the future, to developments which are likely to be seen over the next ten and possibly 20 years. A comparatively new feature of this second edition is the increased consideration of foreign equipment, notably that of Russia and South Africa, which has become possible in open press following world developments in the early-1990s.

Geoffrey Lee, Shrivenham

Acknowledgements

The author would like to acknowledge the considerable work by Brigadier (Retired) J W Ryan Royal Australian Artillery involved in writing the first edition of this book, much of which has formed the basis for this new edition.

The author is also grateful to the following for their considerable advice and assistance in the production of this revised version:

Major General E F G Burton OBE, Assistant Chief of Defence Staff (Operational Requirements) Land

Royal Military College of Science, Shrivenham
    Lieutenant Colonel D H A Blease RA
    Lieutenant Colonel M A Lloyd RWF
    Warrant Officer Class II (SMIG) B C Lane

School of Engineering and Applied Science, Cranfield University, Shrivenham
    Mr M D Bennett

Defence Research Agency, Fort Halstead
    Major T J Price RA

MPM
Shrivenham

Contents

Foreword

Major General E F G Burton OBE
Assistant Chief of Defence Staff (Operational Requirements) Land

The first edition of 'Guns, Mortars and Rockets' provided an invaluable hand book for military students and reference book for Artillery officers. It was clear, concise and basic, and contained a range of self-test questionnaires. This second edition, rewritten by Lieutenant Colonel Michael Manson, formerly a member of the Directing Staff at the Royal Military College of Science, Shrivenham, builds on the strengths of the earlier version and develops the concept of the artillery 'System of Systems'.

The past decade has seen significant improvement in effectiveness in guns, mortars and rockets. Tactical mobility has improved to enable SP guns and rocket launchers to keep up with armoured formations; observers have access to thermal imagers, image intensifiers, laser range finders and target acquisition radars; gun and mortar locating radars, unmanned air vehicles and advanced sound ranging systems are being deployed to locate targets at extended ranges; accuracy is being improved by the measurement of met data at unit level and through improved survey accuracy and muzzle velocity (mv) measurement; MV prediction and the provision of down range met data will follow in due course; the effectiveness of ammunition is being improved continuously through the development of extended range ordnance and charge systems, base bleed and rocket assisted shell, extended range rockets and through the use of a variety of precision munitions.

There is no shortage of technologies as we approach the 21st Century. However, manpower and financial resources are decreasing; Army policy and programming staffs will therefore seek to improve their ability to pick the winners. This requires an understanding of the interaction between the components of the overall artillery system and the cost and benefit of enhancements. The principles are clearly set out in this informative and concise book.

List of Illustrations

All photographs courtesy of RMCS Shrivenham unless otherwise stated.

1

Historical Background

INTRODUCTION

This book is not intended to offer a detailed history of the development of indirect fire weapons or artillery. Many comprehensive volumes have covered this aspect of the subject and some of them are listed in the Bibliography. However, it is useful to study briefly the historical development of artillery in order to understand the reasons for some of the current designs and the sources of certain terminology.

DEFINITIONS

The Glossary near the end of this book provides a comprehensive list of the terminology of indirect fire weapons. But before embarking on a description of how the various platforms evolved, it is worth emphasising the meaning of some of the most fundamental and often misused terms. Unfortunately various developments and misuse have meant that there is now considerable overlap in these meanings.

A Gun

Any device which propels a projectile from a barrel by means of pressure derived from a chemical detonation or burning can be called a gun. The term can thus be applied to a very wide variety of weapons, although those of smaller calibre tend to be known by their specialist names (such as a rifle or a machine-gun) and 'gun' used on its own is now generally understood to refer to weapons of a calibre larger than about 30mm.

A Cannon

Stemming from similar Greek and Latin words meaning a reed or a tube, there is no internationally agreed definition of a cannon but it has been used for any gun larger than a small arm or hand-held weapon. It is often applied to medium calibre (approximately 20 to 50 mm) direct fire weapons, normally with a quick firing capability, as well as to artillery guns of any calibre. It is often used in the USA to refer to artillery guns which only fire in the low angle (less than 45 degrees or 800 mils from horizontal).

A Howitzer

Derived from the German word *haubitze* and invented by the Dutch in the 17th century, a howitzer was lighter and more mobile than a cannon of similar calibre and was designed to fire a large, heavy projectile in the high angle (i.e. above 45 degrees/800 mils). The term is generally used in modern parlance to denote artillery guns which can fire in the high angle.

A Mortar

In its traditional form a mortar is a muzzle-loaded, smooth-bored weapon plat-form designed to fire only in the high angle. The high angle of fire is fundamental and means that the recoil forces can be transmitted directly into the ground so that a recoil mechanism is not required. Mortars without some of these characteristics have been produced, thus leading to confusion in ter-minology; however, any such system that fires in the low angle as well as in the high angle should be termed a 'gun-mortar'. The term was probably derived from the chemist's mortar, since the earliest devices were clumsy, short barrelled weapons resembling this shape.

ORIGINS

The term 'artillery' was originally used to describe mechanical devices which launched projectiles towards a target. Indeed, even in the 16th Century the charter bestowed by Henry VIII upon the Guylde of Saint George (now the Honourable Artillery Company) referred to artillery as 'long bowes, cross bowes and hand gones'. The first mention of gunpowder appears to have been recorded – at least as far as Europe was concerned – in the late 13th Century by Francis Bacon, although it is by no means clear that he invented the com-pound. However, there is no indication that gunpowder was used as a chemical propellant for artillery at the time that he wrote. Cannons were certainly mentioned in the early 14th Century, when such devices used gunpowder to fire either solid shot or arrows. Their effect was almost certainly more psychological than physical, causing terror amongst advancing infantry and cavalry but few casualties due to their inaccuracy and a very slow rate of fire.

CANNONS

The first cannons were cast in bronze and iron, and due to the limitations of metalworking in the early 14th Century they were of quite small calibre. In order to construct barrels of larger dimensions, strips of metal were bound with metal hoops which were then tied around with rope and finally covered with leather. By the late 14th Century cannons capable of firing stones weighing 200lb, and then at least 450lb – equivalent to 22-inch calibre – were in use. These weapons were mainly designed for sieges where their immobility was not a severe limitation. Even so, they still had a very low rate of fire until the idea was born of using several breeches, each one already loaded before being wedged into place at the rear of the barrel in turn. They often proved to be very capable of destroying fortifications and in a wider role they were most beneficial to morale. As a result they were widely adopted by most armies albeit generally in small numbers, since the cost of procurement of both cannon and gunpowder was substantially more than that of funding infantry.

During the 15th Century cannons with trunnions began to appear. These allowed the barrel to be rotated about its point of balance in a vertical plane so that elevation, and hence range, could be adjusted quickly and easily. Such weapons were still only used in the direct fire role where the artilleryman could both fire and also observe the fall of shot. Adjustments to elevation, at first using wedges but by the 16th century using an elevation screw, in order to obtain the correct range, would have been made initially by experience and then trial and error, since the science of ballistics did not begin to evolve until the 17th Century.

Also in the 17th Century the concept developed of using lighter cannons which could be drawn by horses and thus more easily moved around the battlefield, notably by Gustavus Adolphus (1594–1632) of Sweden who employed 4- and 9-pounder (pdr) cannons as well as larger weapons. He constructed barrels by winding wire around a thin metal tube and managed to build a 4pdr cannon weighing 650lb – compared to contemporary 6pdrs weighing around 1,100lb – which could be drawn by one horse and handled by just two men. These allowed artillery to be used not only in sieges, which were becoming less frequent, but also when armies advanced towards each other on an open battlefield. Even so, they were generally brought forward to one position suitable for an opening salvo and were rarely moved in order to correspond to the tactical developments of the battle. In the 18th Century Frederick II the Great (1711–86) of Prussia extended this more mobile concept in the Seven Years' War by forming horse artillery, and in the same era Jean Baptiste de Gribeauval, Inspector General of Artillery in Napoleon's army, grouped artillery resources into coastal/garrison, siege and field. The term 'field' was used to denote 12pdr guns which were moved by horse and supported by limber wagons containing ammunition and spares. Nevertheless, these weapons were still relatively crude, with muzzle loading, a smooth bore and no recoil mechanism.

RIFLING

In the second half of the 19th Century gun design improved swiftly. The value of rifling had been recognised and applied first to small arms, which meant that artillery – still very much a direct fire weapon – became vulnerable to infantry at much longer ranges than, say, the 300 metres of Waterloo. Rifling was then applied to field artillery and was first used by the French in the Italian campaign in the mid-19th Century, and subsequently in all artillery guns since it provided far better accuracy, especially at long ranges. Variations in rifling have been developed over the years: initially a uniform twist was used, then an increasing twist was applied; however, more recently uniform twist has returned since it imposes lower total stresses on the driving band of the shell.

OBTURATION

Obturation is the term used to describe the seal required to constrain the pressure of the ignited charge until the munition leaves the barrel. Although loading at the breech had been used for the earliest cannons this was due to the limitations of the manufacturing process rather than through operational choice. Once barrels could be cast with a closed breech end and the power of the charge had increased in order to provide greater range and to fire larger projectiles, muzzle loading became the norm. However, the gunners involved in muzzle loading were more vulnerable to small arms fire, and loading a rifled gun from the muzzle presented obvious difficulties, although several successful designs were produced. The need for loading at the breech was obvious and by the end of the 19th Century all guns used this system. Once it became feasible to manufacture an opening breech which could also contain the rearward pressure of the firing charge there was, however, considerable debate as to whether Quick Firing (QF) or Breech Loading (BL) was the most suitable obturation system to use. Indeed, only in recent years with the latest breech designs has the argument swung firmly in favour of BL. These systems are described in detail in Chapter 5, but basically a QF system is one where rearward obturation is provided by a cartridge case, while BL involves a seal made by the breech itself fitting into the end of the barrel, the charge or cartridge having no case around it. During most of the 20th Century QF has generally been used for smaller calibres (up to about 120mm) since such cartridge cases are not too heavy, the mechanism allowed a faster rate of fire, and the lighter weight of a QF breech has often been a significant design consideration. Conversely, BL has been used for larger calibres, where a cartridge case would be difficult to manhandle and the breech has been a much smaller proportion of the overall weight.

RECOIL MECHANISMS

Until the end of the 19th Century the problem of constraining recoil had not been solved, and guns were largely free to move backwards as they fired. Consequently, they had to be manhandled back into position after each round, which did not help accuracy, consistency or rate of fire. The first successful recoil system was a hydro-pneumatic mechanism designed by the French which was incorporated in their M1897 75mm field gun, pictured in Figure 1.1. This included the basic elements of a modern system: a hydraulic brake which absorbed the recoil energy and a cylinder in which air was compressed to act as a spring for returning the barrel to its original position. Nevertheless, the M1897 still used brake blocks, positioned beneath the wheels, to assist in the restraint of movement.

SIGHTS

Until the end of the 19th Century artillery was essentially a direct fire weapon and sights tended to be rudimentary. The main requirement was to set the

Figure 1.1 The French M1897 75mm Field Gun

range as accurately as possible and this was usually achieved from the 16th Century onwards by the gunner's quadrant. This device was marked off in points, placed in the bore of the gun and the barrel was elevated until a plumb bob indicated the correct number of points, the latter having been determined through calibration by trial.

However, following the Boer and Russo-Japanese Wars, in which gunners were often picked off by snipers, the need for indirect fire from concealed positions was realised. A tangent sight to set elevation (for range) had been in use since the early 19th Century, but for indirect fire a means of pointing the gun in the correct direction was also required. This was provided from the late 19th Century by the dial sight, which used the bearing to a distant reference object (normally to the rear or to one side of the gun) as a basis for setting the angle to the target.

Thus by the turn of the 20th Century all the basic components of the modern gun were available to a designer: rifling, breech obturation, recoil mechanisms and indirect fire sights. Guns could be designed to fire large projectiles accurately out to long ranges from concealed locations, and their size and weight were largely determined by the level of mobility required.

GIANT GUNS

The potential power of artillery has given rise at various times to the design of massive guns, normally when battles have become mainly static. Long range and projectile size have been maximised when believed necessary. The following two examples indicate what is possible.

Just prior to the First World War the Germans began to develop their 'Big Bertha' series of guns which were initially required to bombard forts. By 1918 the later versions had been designed to fire at Paris. These varied in calibre from 8.26 inches to 15 inches and one fired a 228 pound (about 100kg) shell to a range of about 68 miles (about 100km). It was mounted on a railway line and ammunition was supplied by that means. Its accuracy was not great at maximum range but since the target was central Paris and its aim was to demoralise as much as to cause destruction, it was adequate. Indeed, the shell only contained 7kg of explosive so damage and injuries were relatively light, but its psychological effect was great.

In 1941–42 the Germans went for size rather than range, at the sieges of Sevastopol and Leningrad. They developed the Swere Gustav which had a calibre of 80cm. It fired a 7.5 ton shell to about 28 miles, normally two or three times a day. The guns took three weeks to erect, had a barrel life of some 100 rounds and were manned by a total detachment of 1,500 men commanded by a major general.

Such guns were in some respects the zenith of the design of artillery. It seems most unlikely that such weapons will be seen in action again, since long range and high payloads can now be more easily achieved by rockets and missiles. Nevertheless, Project Babylon, better known as the Iraqi Super Gun, was begun in the late-1980s under the direction of the late Dr Gerald Bull. There were two elements to this. Baby Babylon was a 350mm railway gun firing 155mm two stage base bleed shells with sabots to perhaps 100km range. Big Babylon was a one metre calibre fixed system weighing about 5,000 tons and with an estimated 750km range. It is not thought to have been intended for surface bombardment since its orientation was ideal for inserting objects into polar orbit, but in any case it was never completed.

MORTARS

Mortars were evident amongst the first indirect fire weapons. Their relatively simple design without the need to allow for significant recoil, especially in a horizontal direction, meant that they could be more easily constructed and operated. Moreover, their high trajectory gave them a tactical advantage for use in a siege, where they could be employed more effectively than cannons to lob bombs over fortifications and on top of defenders concealed behind them. Consequently, mortars with very large calibres – of 13 inches and more – were quickly developed.

By the 17th Century mortars of 4.5 inches to 18 inches calibre, normally cast in bronze, were in use. They were often permanently fixed to a baseplate and set at an elevation of 45 degrees, their range variation being achieved by variation in the size of charge. By the late 18th Century mortar bombs with fuzes – which had to be ignited just before the charge – were available. These devices were still very short, the barrel being rarely more than three calibres in length. The largest mortar recorded was Mallet's Mortar, designed in 1854 for the Crimean War, principally for a siege such as that of Sevastopol. It had a calibre of 36 inches and weighed 42 tons, although its ingenious construction meant that no single part weighed more than 12 tons, and it fired projectiles of up to 2,940lb containing 480lb of gunpowder. However, production difficulties prevented the start of trials until three years later – a year after the War had ended – and it never saw active service.

The modern 'stove-pipe' form of mortar was originally designed for the First World War by both the Germans and British. In the largely static trench warfare the value of a light weapon which could be easily carried by the infantry became apparent. The British Army had calibres of 3 inches (the Stokes Mortar), 4 and 6 inches. By the Second World War these had changed to 2, 3 and 4.2 inches and the largest of these fired a 20lb fin–stabilised bomb to a maximum range of 4,100 yards. The United States Army also had a 4.2 inch mortar but it was rifled and so used spin, rather than fin, stabilisation. Modern mortars have fundamentally changed little since these designs were produced.

ROCKETS

Rockets existed in China possibly before the 10th Century; they were mainly used as pyrotechnic devices for fireworks, although both the Chinese and the Arabs of the 13th Century used them as rudimentary incendiary weapons. Similar weapons were also in use in Europe in the 14th Century but they had very limited effect and the development of cannons proved to be more promising. By the late 17th Century detailed instructions for the construction of rockets as fireworks were available but although some efforts were made to establish them as weapons in various armies, they did not reappear as a significant weapon until the end of the 18th Century. At the siege of Seringapatam in India in 1799 rockets 8 inches in length and 1.5 inches in diameter with an explosive warhead were used by Tipu Sultan to some effect.

However, it was Colonel Sir William Congreve who, in 1804, began to produce viable rockets. He recognised the advantages of virtually no recoil, allowing simple launchers, and light overall weight which allowed their use as long-range weapons even by lightly equipped forces, advantages which are still pertinent today. His developments over the next few years produced weapons with longer ranges than most cannons of the day while achieving comparable accuracy. Gradually he developed rockets with ranges of 500 yards, then 1,500 yards, then the 6pdr (total weight) with a range of 2,000 yards. Perhaps his most successful device was the 32pdr, a rocket with an iron case, an incendiary warhead equivalent to that of a 10 inch cannon and a range of 3,000 yards. It is worth noting that the range of the 10 inch cannon at that time was only about 2,000 yards. Congreve also developed a wide range of warheads: explosive, case shot, shrapnel and shells. His rockets were successfully used in various engagements in the early 19th Century including Boulogne, Copenhagen and Leipzig – where O Battery (The Rocket Troop) Royal Artillery acquired their honour title. Various designers continued Congreve's work during the first half of the 19th Century, culminating with an effective demonstration by William Hale of the Royal Arsenal of rockets using deflected thrust to impart longitudinal rotation and thus enhance stability and accuracy. However, there were still problems with corrosion, windage and the movement of the rocket's centre of gravity as the propellant burnt which limited usefulness, and by 1870 the rifled gun was proving to be a much more effective weapon platform.

Some 60 years later in the 1930s German research was becoming very successful. In 1933 the A1 appeared: it was 4.5 feet long, one foot in diameter and weighed 330lb. The programme led eventually to the A4 (designated the V2 by the Allies) which was 46 feet long, 5.5 feet in diameter and weighed 12.5 tons. Of this weight, about two-thirds was fuel – a mixture of ethyl alcohol and liquid oxygen – and the warhead was 2,150lb of amatol. The motor burnt for one minute, the time of flight was four minutes, vertex height was 60 miles and the range was 180 to 220 miles. It was of course a most effective strategic weapon and became the forerunner of most of the major rocket systems of the Cold War, since members of the design team were quickly moved to the USA or Russia as soon as the Second World War ended.

CONCLUSION

This chapter has charted an outline of some significant developments in technology which have brought artillery to its current position. As with so many areas of human progress, artillery has developed faster in the 20th Century than in any previous period. It has seen the transfer of artillery from a direct fire role to one of predominantly indirect fire. This ability to attack from a position of relative security is increasingly important in modern warfare. In turn this suggests that artillery will continue to be a key weapon system and will therefore continue to be developed well into the 21st Century. Some ideas of how that will and might happen are discussed in Chapter 7.

2

Indirect Fire Systems

A SYSTEMS APPROACH

It is important to emphasise that indirect fire should always be considered as a system involving five elements: target location, C^4 (command, control, communication and computation), munitions, weapon platforms and logistics. The system will only be as good as the weakest of these elements. For example, increasing weapon range is only worthwhile if targets can be located in time to be engaged at the maximum range. Similarly, increasing the rate at which a weapon can be fired is likely to require commensurate improvements in the supporting logistic system in order to provide ammunition at an adequate rate. The complexity of this whole system generally varies with the weapon platform: for a mortar it can be quite simple; for a rocket launcher it will normally involve several expensive sub-systems. A diagram indicating the various elements of the whole system is at Figure 2.1.

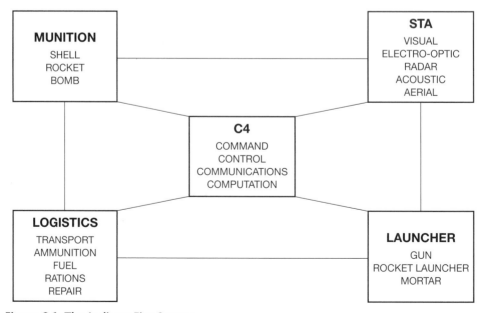

Figure 2.1 The Indirect Fire System

This book concentrates primarily on the weapon platform and to a lesser extent on the munitions. Other books in the Brassey's series describe and discuss the remaining aspects of the indirect fire system in similar detail. However, the relationship between the five elements must be so close that a brief résumé of them is appropriate here. But first one must consider the operational context within which indirect fire is usually employed.

OPERATIONAL CONCEPTS

When considering the application of technology to indirect fire weapon systems, the two fundamental concepts for their use on the battlefield should be borne in mind. Terminology in this area can differ between countries and can change with time, but it is the underlying concepts that are unlikely to change that are important.

Close Support

Indirect Fire is required to provide Close Support to other combat forces, to attack targets of immediate concern to battlegroups and brigades. These are the front-line forces in what is often termed the contact battle. To be effective, the response time must be fast, fire must be accurate because it may be brought down very close to own forces, and ideally it should defeat all types of targets or at least neutralise them.

Depth Fire

Indirect Fire is also, and often simultaneously, required to attack targets in depth in order to prevent enemy follow-on or reserve forces from reinforcing or influencing the contact battle. Compared to Close Support, Depth Fire system response time could often afford to be slower, especially for static targets; accuracy might acceptably be less; and targets will often be less well protected. However, many recent technological developments have begun to increase aspirations in this area: for example long-range precision targeting of armoured vehicles and other high value targets is seen as an important future capability.

SURVEILLANCE AND TARGET ACQUISITION

Surveillance and Target Acquisition (STA) must be matched to the range at which the indirect fire system is operating and the type of operations in which it is engaged. The STA system will generally need a 24 hour, all-weather capability, since this is normally quoted as a strong advantage of indirect fire weapons themselves.

For Close Support, indirect fire will often be applied at the earliest opportunity. If possible, this requires detection beyond the line of sight from the observer with forward troops to the target in order to provide warning. Subsequently, at least target recognition and location at the limits of line of sight are required, from which point accurate engagement may well begin. Thus the STA system will probably be a mixture of technologies: perhaps remote sensors such as unmanned aircraft with links to forward troops for warning, and high resolution sensors working in the visual and infra-red wavebands for recognition and location.

For Depth Fire, indirect viewing and/or target location will normally be required. Non-visual characteristics of the target will often be exploited. These will include electronic and thermal signatures, acoustics and ballistic trajectory (when considering counter-battery fire against mortars, guns and rockets). Airborne sensors such as manned aircraft with photographic pods or radars and unmanned aircraft, together with ground-based sensors such as radars and manned reconnaissance, are likely to predominate. Ideally they should provide a real-time link to command centres and thence to weapon platforms in order to minimise engagement times and allow mobile targets to be hit.

Further details of these systems can be found in Volume 4 of this Brassey's series[1].

C^4

The nature of indirect fire, especially artillery, with its long ranges and potential wide influence and flexibility on the battlefield means that C^4 will normally be more complex than for a direct fire formation of comparable size.

An artillery unit might typically have a range of at least 20km, compared to the 2km range of a tank or medium range anti-tank guided weapon. This provides a regiment of three or four batteries, totalling up to 32 guns, with adequate range to fire deep into the enemy's reserves and, just as importantly, in front of several brigades and even divisions to the flanks. This large range coverage will generally result in command being retained at high levels in order to maximise overall effectiveness.

Conversely, the need for a fast speed of response between the identification of targets and their engagement will normally require control to be exercised at low level, for example by mortar fire controllers, forward observation officers, or weapon locating radars. Low level control will allow precise judgement in the timing of engagements and also for quick adjustment of fire as the tactical situation develops.

In order to link the high level command and the low level control, communications will almost invariably be by some form of radio link, unless the situation is static and troops have had time to lay telephone cable to enhance security. Once again, a good speed of response will require links to be as direct as possible, whichever means of transmission is employed. Fortunately, modern communications, often controlled by computers, can provide quick switching to enable direct links to be created instantly.

Computation for indirect fire systems has two aspects: firstly the need to produce an accurate ballistic solution for the weapon platform; and secondly the ability to assist with battle management, i.e. command, control and communications. It is obvious that all elements of the C^4 system need to be closely integrated to provide the most efficient solution, and this has been the driving force behind the development of systems such as the Battlefield Artillery Target Engagement System (BATES) deployed with the British Army and the Army Field Artillery Target Direction System (AFATDS) deployed with US forces. Further discussion of these systems can be found in Volumes 5 and 12 of the 2nd Brassey's Land Warfare series [2,3].

WEAPON PLATFORMS

It is important to remember that the indirect fire weapon is the mortar bomb, or shell, or rocket. The mortar, gun or rocket launcher is the means of firing the weapon towards the target, and to a large extent their design is independent of the targets to be engaged. Advantages and disadvantages of indirect fire weapon platforms are discussed in Chapter 3. It should be noted that a robust system should contain all three types of platform, since their respective advantages are complementary and serve to overcome the disadvantages of each.

MUNITIONS

All weapons should be designed primarily to defeat the specified target. Since there is such a wide range of indirect fire targets – increasingly any type of target within range – this means that there needs to be a wide variety of munitions each optimised for a particular task. In general terms these tasks or types of fire are, in increasing order of effect: harassment, neutralisation, attrition and destruction, terms which are discussed in Chapter 3. Achieving greater effects normally implies the need for larger quantities of ammunition, so in order to reduce logistic burdens 'improved conventional' and 'smart' munitions, with much higher individual kill probabilities, are being developed.

The basic high explosive shell or bomb is still the mainstay of gun and mortar ammunition stocks. It is relatively cheap, reliable, simple to use and effective against a very wide range of targets. However, improved conventional munitions, notably shells filled with bomblets, are often far more effective against certain targets, since they can provide greater saturation of the target area and can penetrate armour more effectively. The US M483 bomblet shell, as an example, contains 88 bomblets of the type shown in Figure 2.2.

It can be seen that the bomblet not only has a fragmentation effect horizontally, which will cause injuries and fatalities to personnel, but it also has a shaped charge warhead which will penetrate the armour of many fighting vehicles. The 88 bomblets spread out over a wide area after being ejected from the shell in the air, whereas a single HE shell will have its effect concentrated around its point of burst. Small calibre weapons, such as mortars and 105mm guns, are less likely to use bomblet munitions since each round cannot contain a useful number of bomblets. Conversely, most rocket systems are far more likely to use them because the large number carried will cover a much greater area than a single HE warhead of equivalent volume.

Another form of improved munition is the minelet. Here, the shell or rocket ejects several submunitions by air-burst and they fall to the ground on a small parachute. Once they hit the ground they self-activate and use advanced sensors to fire a shaped charge warhead through the belly of an armoured vehicle

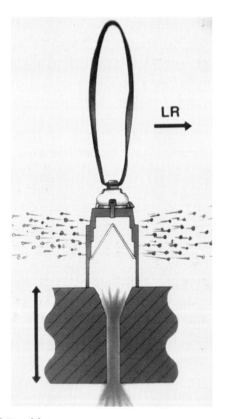

Figure 2.2   A Typical Bomblet

passing above them. Such remotely delivered minefields are quick to lay and can be very effective, especially when used temporarily to halt or channel an enemy force so that it can be attacked more easily by artillery, aircraft, attack helicopters or manoeuvre forces.

A possible improved conventional weapon which has many attractions but which has proved difficult to develop successfully is the fuel-air explosive shell or rocket. The principle here is to burst the warhead container and create a cloud of fuel droplets in the air. Once created, the cloud is detonated by a delayed fuze and a very high pressure pulse is achieved over a large area. This pressure would certainly cause significant casualties to troops, and an alternative role could be to explode pressure–sensitive mines – thus creating a gap in a minefield. Development problems seem to have centred on the ability to achieve the correct fuel–air ratio throughout the desired target area, and on detonating the mixture at the optimum time. Nevertheless, the Russian Army at least is understood to have an operational warhead of this type.

Turning to weapons of mass destruction, nuclear and chemical warheads have been developed and fielded for launch by both guns and rockets. It is likely that biological warheads have at least been designed as well. The attraction of using artillery to deliver such munitions is obvious, since they must be fired at long range in order to avoid own force casualties. Whether such weapons will remain in the inventories of some armies is questionable, but despite the likelihood of global bans on them it would be naïve not to think that some nations will keep stocks in secret.

As subsidiary tasks, smoke and illumination may also be required from an indirect fire system. A modern shell of 155mm calibre can provide a very effective smoke screen which lasts for up to several minutes or it can contain a parachute flare which will illuminate an area of about one square kilometre for over a minute. The advent of thermal imagers which can see through normal smoke and do not need illumination to function at night is reducing the need for these munitions, but until every soldier is equipped with such visual aids they are still likely to be required. Furthermore, the worldwide proliferation of thermal imagers has led to a requirement for smoke which can obscure in both the visual and infra-red wavelengths.

Some discussion of ammunition is included in the chapters concerning each type of weapon platform, and current and future developments are considered in Chapter 7, but much more detail can be found in Volume 4 of the 2nd Brassey's Land Warfare series[4].

LOGISTICS

Typically around 75% of the logistic effort for a mechanised force at war will be devoted to the resupply of indirect fire munitions. The logistic system must be flexible and robust, and will need to make use of *matériel* handling aids at all levels to improve speed and minimise manpower.

There are normally two distinct aspects to the ammunition resupply system, and they tend to require very different transport solutions. The first is the movement of stocks from supply dumps to the artillery area. This is likely to involve rapid road movement over long distances and the carriage of large volumes of ammunition on each vehicle for efficiency. The second problem is the movement of smaller quantities of munitions over a much shorter distance from the logistic vehicle to the mortar, gun or rocket launcher.

A good solution to the first problem is the British Dismountable Rack Offloading and Pickup System (DROPS), shown in Figure 2.3, which can load, move and unload large quantities of ammunition rapidly. It uses a hydraulically operated hook on the vehicle to pick up a flatrack, which might contain 170 complete rounds of 155mm ammunition or 24 Multiple Launch Rocket System (MLRS) rockets, within two minutes. Being a wheeled vehicle it can move at high speed on roads and tracks, and to some extent across country as well, to a dumping position where it unloads the flatrack, again within two minutes. This operation is far faster than a normal lorry with auxiliary load handling equipment could manage, and by dumping the ammunition at ground level the handling problem at the destination is reduced.

The second logistic problem is the efficient transfer of ammunition from resupply vehicles to the turret or chamber of the gun, or to the rocket launcher. Depending on where the rounds have been dumped, there may be a need for load handling equipment such as a fork-lift truck to carry pallets or containers of ammunition to the rear of the gun. For towed guns and small calibre rockets the simplest and cheapest method of loading is then to manhandle the shells or rockets and load them. 155mm shells, which weigh over 40kg,

Figure 2.3 DROPS

will be tiring and slow to replenish in large volumes, particularly within the confined space of a self-propelled gun. One solution, adopted by the US Army, is to use a tracked limber vehicle with mechanical assistance which deploys behind an M109 self-propelled (SP) gun. This also has the advantage of protecting the ammunition handlers, but it cannot carry the same quantity of rounds as a DROPS truck, for example. Consequently its own replenishment becomes an extra task.

Another idea which has been considered is to tow a trailer behind the gun. This does not obviate the need for manual ammunition handling, but it does provide a large, immediately available supply of rounds close to the gun. However, towing a wheeled trailer behind a tracked gun can reduce tactical mobility, especially in confined spaces.

Larger calibre shells (above 155mm) and most rockets will certainly be too heavy for manual handling and so require mechanical loading, a good example being the MLRS which has a boom crane loading system built into the launcher.

Self-propelled guns have the design option of automatic or semi-automatic loading, as well as using simple manual loading. Some mechanical systems are outlined in Chapter 5.

SUMMARY

This chapter has emphasised the close interdependence of the five elements of the indirect fire system. Higher system effectiveness can be achieved by a development in one area, but related improvements in one or more of the other areas will usually provide an even better overall result. This process is therefore a synergistic one. It is a theme that will be taken up again in Chapter 7 when discussing future trends.

NOTES

[1] M.A. Richardson *et al.*, '*Surveillance and Target Acquisition Systems*', Brassey's, London (1996)
[2] M.A. Rice and A.J. Sammes, '*Communications and Information Systems for Battlefield Command and Control*', Brassey's, London (1989)
[3] M.A. Rice and A.J. Sammes, '*Command and Control Support Systems in the Gulf War*', Brassey's, London (1994)
[4] P.R. Courtney-Green, '*Ammunition for the Land Battle*', Brassey's, London (1991)

3

Comparison of Weapon Launchers

INTRODUCTION

Modern artillery systems, including mortars, exist to provide indirect fire onto targets. Guns and some types of mortar may have a limited capability for direct fire, but this is always a secondary consideration. Apart from needing a direct fire sight, the design of the equipment is unlikely to be significantly affected by direct fire considerations.

The design features of the weapon launcher are influenced firstly by the munition that is to be fired and the range, accuracy and rate of fire to be achieved. The nature of the operational environment in which the system will be used is also highly significant. However, the ending of the Cold War – a major international influence on weapon system design – has left many armies with large quantities of equipment designed for a major armoured or mechanised battle. This legacy, combined with the reduced size of modern armies, suggests that most systems might be expected to operate in almost any circumstance. Nevertheless, a balance will usually have to be struck between the levels of firepower, mobility and protection that are acceptable. These factors will be discussed later in this chapter. It is inevitable that the final design will be a compromise of many characteristics, and also that no single system will meet the full range of indirect fire tasks. Hence most armies will require a family of weapon launchers and munitions.

INDIRECT FIRE TASKS

Having discussed the operational concepts of close support and depth fire in Chapter 2, it is worth considering the tasks of indirect fire before examining the characteristics of the various weapon launchers, which in turn will lead to their design. The terminology that follows is in use in most Western countries and although definitions may vary slightly the general meanings should be understood throughout the world.

Harassment

Harassment is not expected to cause significant *matériel* damage. It is employed speculatively to have a detrimental effect on morale and the physiological condition of enemy troops by disrupting their work, their freedom of movement and their rest. It is usually carried out at long range using low rates of fire, perhaps at irregular intervals over a protracted period, and when accurate and timely target acquisition is not available.

Neutralisation

The effects of neutralisation cover a wide spectrum. Although it might occasionally be seen as a purely indirect fire task, neutralisation is normally used in conjunction with the fire and manoeuvre of other forces – such as infantry, armour and aviation – to hamper and interrupt enemy movement and/or the firing of enemy weapons. Enemy casualties of up to 30% might be required or expected, in order that friendly forces can carry out their mission more effectively. An initial, heavy burst of accurate fire is required, probably followed by sustained fire for many minutes at a lower rate.

Attrition

Attrition is a rather more deliberate attempt than neutralisation to deplete enemy combat power significantly. Specific important soft or semi-armoured targets such as communications centres will be selected because a high guarantee of destruction can be given. Once again a heavy burst of fire over a few seconds will be most effective, but subsequent sustained fire will not normally be used.

Destruction

The term destruction, when used in indirect fire, implies that a target will be put out of action permanently. Usually, heavy rates of accurate fire will be used and will continue until destruction is certain. Such fire requires very large quantities of standard High Explosive (HE) or bomblet ammunition, but the development of precision munitions would have a significant impact on achieving this task and make it more suitable for artillery.

It is now appropriate to consider some common requirements of weapon launchers, before proceeding to compare the characteristics of mortars, guns and rockets in turn. This overview then leads into chapters describing the technology of each launcher platform in detail.

RANGE

The Need for Long Range

A major characteristic of all indirect fire systems is long range, and this provides their inherent flexibility. There are many reasons to strive for long range. The first is that it allows the concentration of more weapons onto a given target in order to provide a heavier weight of fire, surprise and shock action. Secondly, greater range permits the engagement of targets further into the depth and flanks of an enemy force. Alternatively, it could allow the weapon launcher to fire from a position of greater security further behind friendly force lines: it reduces the chance that the launcher will be engaged by armour, infantry or artillery; and it might allow the launcher to remain in one position for longer and thus be more readily available to fire. Long range is becoming increasingly important on modern 'dispersed' battlefields.

Increasing Range

Range can be increased by modifying the launcher, the munition, the propellant or all three. Launcher modifications are discussed in the following chapters, but in summary they involve the use of longer barrels, larger chamber size and/or better propellants to generate more firing energy.

Modifications to the munition can be divided into those which improve its ballistic coefficient – and hence reduce drag – and those which provide a post-firing boost. Drag can be reduced by streamlining the munition, but this is likely to be at the expense of reducing its target effectiveness since there will be less volume in which to carry HE or submunitions.

A base bleed unit fitted to a shell fills the turbulent, partial vacuum behind the projectile in flight with gas bled from a small generator, thereby decreasing base drag and improving aerodynamics. The unit can increase range by up to 25%, but it would take up about 10% of the internal volume, thus reducing payload, unless it can be screwed onto the base of the shell. A post-firing boost can be provided by fitting a small rocket unit into the shell or bomb, this complete package being known as a Rocket Assisted Projectile (RAP). Although this will provide the greatest enhancement to range it also has the greatest penalty in terms of payload reduction, typically taking up about 25% of the internal volume. RAP are in service with the US and Russian armies, and possibly some others. It should be noted that base bleed and rocket assistance (especially) both decrease accuracy and consistency, yet further reducing target effectiveness.

Range Coverage

If a gun had a single propellant charge, large enough to achieve the required maximum range, it would have problems engaging targets at short and medium ranges. The high muzzle velocity would lead to high muzzle wear and would also mean that the trajectory would have to be very low and so the shell might hit any intervening high ground. Alternatively, the gun would have to fire in the high angle, but this would make it more detectable by radars and would decrease accuracy since it would be increasingly affected by meteorological conditions. A second problem is that a slight error in the elevation of the barrel would have a significant effect on the impact point, so accuracy and consistency would be degraded. Mortars with only one charge would also suffer from this second problem, although not so much from the first since they fire in the high angle anyway.

Consequently, in order to provide good range coverage – i.e. short minimum range and long maximum range – while maintaining accuracy, mortars and guns employ different amounts of propellant to vary the muzzle velocity. This is not normally possible for rockets and leads to one of their disadvantages. Finite differences in charge sizes must be used, at least for solid propellant, since measuring the amount of charge before it is loaded is obviously not practical. The number of different charges will be a compromise between the need for accuracy between minimum and maximum range, and the need to minimise complexity for the detachment, or an autoloader if that is to be used. Typically, mortars use about five charges and guns use about eight.

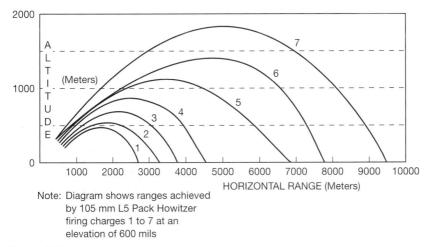

Note: Diagram shows ranges achieved by 105 mm L5 Pack Howitzer firing charges 1 to 7 at an elevation of 600 mils

Figure 3.1 Range Coverage

A possible problem for guns with long range is that because the chamber must be large enough to accommodate the highest charge, the smallest desired charge may be unable to generate sufficient pressure to push the projectile out of the barrel. Thus either a longer minimum range must be accepted, with tactical penalties, or the lowest charge must be made from a propellant mixture with different burning characteristics.

ACCURACY AND CONSISTENCY

Indirect fire is normally employed to attack area targets and therefore some degree of dispersion is desired. Nonetheless, accuracy and consistency are important since they determine the time and the quantity of ammunition needed to attack a target effectively.

Definitions

Accuracy is a measure of the precision with which the mean point of impact (MPI) of a group of rounds can be placed on the target. Consistency is a measure of the spread of the rounds about the MPI when each is aimed at the same target. Combinations of good and poor accuracy and consistency are shown in Figure 3.2.

Accuracy should be considered as a function of the overall indirect fire system, so it is affected by many sources of error, including survey of the guns, target location, ammunition variations, instrument precision, meteorology and

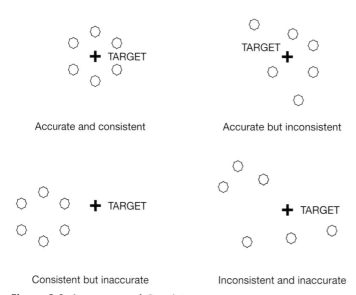

Accurate and consistent   Accurate but inconsistent

Consistent but inaccurate   Inconsistent and inaccurate

Figure 3.2 Accuracy and Consistency

operator error. Consistency is affected by round to round variations in factors such as muzzle velocity, meteorology, sight setting and laying, and ramming.

Consistency, or the dispersion plus and minus of the MPI, is a statistical function and therefore predictable, and is shown in Figure 3.3. Note that a similar dispersion will apply either side of the line of fire, although this is usually smaller. The area over which a given percentage of rounds will land will theoretically be an oval.

The PE_r and its equivalent for line, the PE_l, have two major uses. Firstly, they allow observers and planning staffs to calculate the area that will be covered by the projectiles arriving at the target. Secondly, they allow an observer, who is adjusting fire onto a target, to know when there is no point in making further corrections because any misses are merely dispersion due to inconsistency.

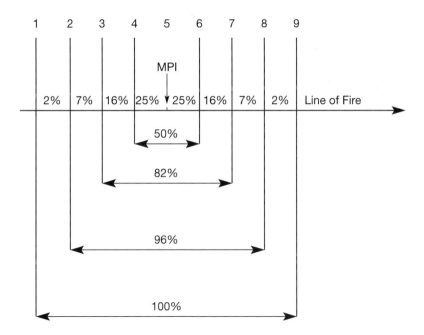

Note: 1. 50% of rounds fired will probably fall between lines 4 and 6, 82% between lines 3 and 7 and so on.

2. An alternative explanation of the diagram is that if a single round is fired it has 50% chance of falling between lines 4 and 6.

3. The distance between adjacent vertical lines is equal and for a given charge varies with range. It is known as the 'Probable Error Range' (PE_r)

Figure 3.3 Dispersion

Another factor affecting the dispersion of rounds at the target can be the spread of the guns or mortars at their firing position. Until recently it was normal to fire each gun on the same bearing ('lines of fire parallel') or with the bearings 'converged' so that each projectile was aimed at exactly the same point. However, modern ballistic computing is fast enough to predict a separate bearing and elevation for each gun, so that the individual points of aim cover the specified target dimensions and orientation in the optimum way.

While some dispersion (inconsistency) is normally desirable in a system that is designed to attack area targets, perfect accuracy is highly desirable, if unattainable. Improved accuracy minimises the time taken to hit the target effectively and also reduces the number of rounds needed to do so. For a given charge, accuracy will always be less at longer ranges because a slight difference between the true and applied bearing and elevation, and the greater effect of meteorological conditions, will result in greater displacement between the MPI and the target.

Terminal Guidance

Terminally guided munitions, which are mainly discussed in Chapter 7, still require a reasonable level of accuracy and consistency since their seeker will have a finite field of view. For example, if a seeker head in a shell or bomb has a 300 metre diameter field of view, but the total error at the target is 500 metres, it is possible that the seeker will not be able to detect the target and home onto it.

MOBILITY

As mentioned earlier in this chapter, mobility is one of the prime considerations in the overall design of indirect fire launchers, because a given degree of mobility demands a compromise on other characteristics. This degree will be influenced by the nature of operations in which the launcher will be employed, and by the mobility of other components of the force. The key criterion is that the launcher must be able to deploy, or be deployed, into such a position that it can carry out its task as part of that force. Three levels of mobility need to be considered.

Strategic Mobility

Strategic mobility concerns deployability to a theatre of operations. External dimensions will be important here, to ensure that the equipment can fit into an aircraft, a landing craft or the hold of a ship, or that it is within rail gauges. If portability by air is important then weight will also be a key factor at this level.

Operational Mobility

Operational mobility concerns redeployability over relatively long distances within a theatre of operations. Weight is likely to be the key factor here, especially if the equipment needs to be carried under a medium support helicopter. Dimensions will be constrained to ensure that movement on a tank transporter is possible, but this is unlikely to be a more stringent requirement than that for strategic mobility. It is worth noting that a self-propelled gun has an inherent disadvantage in that if it breaks down, its firepower is, temporarily at least, lost. If the towing vehicle for a towed gun breaks down, another vehicle will normally be available to take over immediately.

Tactical Mobility

Tactical mobility concerns movement on the battlefield itself. A gun, mortar or rocket launcher does not necessarily need the same level of mobility as the infantry or armour with which it may operate. For example, a self-propelled gun is unlikely to need similar agility – the ability to move between fire positions quickly – as a tank or infantry fighting vehicle, because its range usually allows it to avoid being in the direct fire battle area. Consequently, its engine power to vehicle weight ratio can be less and its transmission and suspension systems can be of lower specification. Low weight could be a significant advantage in some situations since it allows movement across a wider range of bridges. Once again, movement of towed guns by helicopter may have to be considered here. For example, in the Falklands Campaign of 1982 cross-country vehicle movement was often impossible so most redeployments of the British 105mm Light Guns were performed by helicopters. Some medium towed guns such as the FH70 and the South African G5 have auxiliary motors to provide local mobility and powered assistance for deployment, although at best this reduces airportability and can eliminate carriage by most helicopters.

Design Factors Affecting Mobility

In addition to the required levels of mobility and the nature of the equipment's task, the mass of the projectile, its maximum range and any detachment protection will all influence mobility. A heavy projectile and/or a long range will generate large firing stresses which guns and mortars must withstand while remaining stable. Rockets are not affected in this way, as discussed later. Muzzle brakes can be used to reduce recoil forces but their efficiency must be limited on towed guns to avoid excessive blast overpressures which would damage the detachment. Light alloys with a high strength to weight ratio can be used, but they can be difficult and expensive to fabricate and repair.

PROTECTION

The main threats to artillery and mortars come from indirect fire weapons, attack helicopters and ground attack aircraft. Most air-launched guided weapons and rockets are designed to defeat tank armour, and a gun, mortar or rocket launcher cannot hope to have better protection than a tank. Consequently they must use tactical methods to counteract these threats, such as dispersion, concealment, digging, camouflage and mobility. However, they may be able to include sufficient protection in their design to withstand the effects of shells and bombs.

Protection for Towed Guns

Shields were the first form of protection included on towed guns, originally fitted for the primary aim of defeating small arms fire from the front when artillery was used in the direct fire role. They also provided some protection against indirect fire from the same direction, but their purpose is defeated by munitions airbursting or landing behind the gun. Their other advantage is that they reduce the effect of the muzzle blast on the detachment. However these advantages are generally considered insufficient when balanced against the modern demand for a light weight in towed guns, and they are rarely used now.

A towed gun is comparatively robust, with the most vulnerable parts of the equipment being the sights and the recoil mechanism. On the FH70 and G5, the motor and the hydraulic lines connecting components to it are also weak points. Some limited degree of armour protection can reduce vulnerability, but accepting the need to replace broken parts is probably more realistic. However, a recoil system can also be given some protection by positioning it under the barrel and ideally in the cradle, where it is less likely to be hit by shell and bomb fragments.

Protection for Self-propelled Guns and Mortars

The design of self-propelled guns and mortars owes more to the need for tactical mobility than protection. Indeed, most early SP guns, developed during the Second World War, were little more than the ordnance of an existing towed gun fitted to a tank or infantry personnel carrier chassis, with hardly any crew protection. As discussed in Chapter 5, large calibre SP guns, such as the 175mm US M107 shown in Figure 3.4, cannot easily be mounted in a turret to provide useful protection for the detachment. However, most modern SP guns, at 152mm or 155mm calibre can readily be fitted inside a turret to give some protection. The level of protection is, like that of a tank, traded off against mobility. The US-designed M109 and the Russian 2S3 both weigh around

26 tons and have marginal protection against shells and small arms fire. Alternatively, the British AS90 can stop fragments from a very near burst of a 155mm shell or small arms fire at point blank range, but it weighs 45 tons.

MORTARS

General Characteristics

Possibly the prime characteristic of a mortar is its simplicity. It is smooth bored, allowing rapid muzzle loading and no requirement for a breech. It does not have a recoil mechanism, the majority of the recoil force being transmitted into the ground through the base plate. Consequently it is normally constrained to fire in the high angle, above 800mils, and cannot be used in the direct fire role.

Although mortars have been designed with rifled barrels and with breeches, such types of equipment are unorthodox and are effectively a cross between a gun and a mortar. Such variations are described in Chapter 4. They confer certain advantages but also disadvantages: a balance which needs to be carefully considered.

Mobility

The simplicity and lower weight of a mortar compared to a gun of similar calibre gives it an advantage in terms of mobility. Mortars up to about 100mm calibre can normally be carried, in a few parts, by a small team of men. Their ammunition is also usually manportable. Consequently in very rough or other

Figure 3.4 M107 Self-propelled gun

Figure 3.5 An 81 mm Mortar and Detachment

difficult terrain a mortar may be the only indirect fire weapon system capable of being deployed unless helicopters are available. They are thus well suited to the close support of infantry, particularly in the dismounted role, and indeed in most armies they are manned by the infantry unless they are of heavy calibre and have long range. However, the weight of ammunition must also be considered. For a given target effect mortars and guns will require broadly equivalent weights and volumes of bombs and shells. The logistic resupply will therefore need to have a similar capability, and for a protracted operation this may well be beyond an infantry battalion.

Ammunition

The smooth bore of a mortar means that bombs cannot easily be spin stabilised and must use fin stabilisation. Since the mortar fires in the high angle, leading to a high altitude for much of the trajectory, the fins may be subjected to considerable meteorological effects. Hence accuracy and consistency will tend to suffer. However, the steep angle of descent tends to give a more even spread of fragments around the MPI compared to a shell, which arrives at a more acute angle to the ground.

Most mortars have subsonic muzzle velocities, so their bombs are subjected to much lower acceleration and pressure in the barrel than shells in a gun. This means that the force on the body of the bomb is lower and so its walls can be thinner than those of a shell. In turn, this permits a larger volume of high explosive to be used in the filling. Furthermore, the bomb walls can be designed for optimum fragmentation without the need to consider strength to withstand high firing stresses. Alternatively, cheaper, lower quality materials can be used in their manufacture.

Range

Mortars have poor maximum range compared to guns and rockets, and the scope for increasing it is limited. A higher bomb velocity would be required. If the mortar itself is modified, the barrel would need to be longer to allow the pressure to act on the bomb for a longer time. Alternatively, it would need to be stronger to contain a higher pressure. Either way, the mortar would be heavier, reducing one of its prime advantages. The bomb could be modified by the addition of a rocket to give it a post-firing boost, and by streamlining, in which case its warhead volume would be reduced. Additionally, the walls of the bomb would have to be thicker to withstand the higher acceleration forces, so they could no longer be optimised for fragmentation. Furthermore, the aerodynamics of supersonic fin-stabilised bombs would not be consistent, and accuracy would suffer.

Even a small increase in muzzle velocity would have its disadvantages. This would put bombs into the transonic velocity regime (around the speed of sound) where aerodynamics become very uncertain, again to the detriment of accuracy. The maximum range theoretically achievable in a vacuum for a bomb fired at 310m/s at 800 mils elevation is about 12km. In practice air drag will reduce this to 9km, and rather less for smaller calibres. Nevertheless, some of the above modifications have been developed by some countries, and they are mentioned in Chapter 4.

Rate of Fire

The ease and speed of muzzle loading a mortar allows it to have an extremely high rate of fire – up to 30 bombs per minute. Initially, the only limitation is the time taken for the bomb to drop down the barrel. However, after a while crew fatigue will set in. The rate of fire will then be limited by the weight of the bomb (and hence its calibre), the length of the barrel, the size of the crew and the availability of ammunition. Nevertheless, unless a gun has a very complex, and therefore expensive, autoloader, it will not approach the intense rate of fire of a mortar.

Protection

Unless a mortar is mounted in an armoured vehicle, it will not have any inherent self-protection. Consequently the crew will either have to dig a pit in the ground and operate from there, or they will have to move regularly. Both operations will take time and thus limit the ability to fire. However, the small size and light weight of a mortar at least make such actions easier and quicker than for a towed gun. It should be noted that protection of some form will be a high priority, because the high trajectory of a mortar bomb makes it very susceptible to detection by radars. Mounting the mortar in an armoured vehicle provides some protection and higher mobility (given suitable terrain), but the loader will still need access around the muzzle and he would still be vulnerable to airburst munitions. Better protection will be obtained if the barrel is mounted in a turret, but then it must be breech loaded, to the detriment of simplicity and rate of fire. Of course, such a complex system will also be expensive.

GUNS

General Characteristics

Considering all the tasks of indirect fire, a gun is the most flexible weapon system to fulfil most of them effectively. They have a wide range coverage, from a few kilometres to tens of kilometres, and are reasonably accurate at all ranges. Modern guns can provide burst rates of fire for shock effect, and then sustained fire at lower rates for considerable periods. They have a fast response time, and a wide range of munition types.

Mobility and Protection

The most obvious feature of a gun is whether it is self-propelled or towed. This choice in design will be determined by the relative importance of the various levels of mobility and of protection that were discussed earlier in this chapter.

Figure 3.6 AS90

Sometimes this may seem obvious: a gun which will deploy with armoured or mechanised forces will almost certainly be SP and will have at least light armour protection; a gun for use with light forces will probably be towed, with little or no protection. However, the wide variety of potential scenarios suggests that this may not always be so simple. An SP gun may be significantly heavier than mechanised infantry vehicles and so be subject to major route restrictions. Consequently, towed guns may have to be deployed instead. A good example here is the deployment of NATO forces in Bosnia in 1995. The French Army were able to find suitable routes for their SP 155mm guns. This was not initially possible in some of the areas in which British troops deployed, so although they had Warrior tracked armoured troop carriers they also deployed with 105mm Light Guns. In general, it seems likely that a rapid reaction force would deploy with towed guns, but SP guns would follow as soon as possible after initial consolidation.

Ammunition

Guns have the widest range of ammunition of all indirect fire launchers. This can be in a variety of calibres, but anything less than 105mm is considered ineffective and anything greater than 155mm is often considered too heavy and cumbersome. The trend in recent years has been to concentrate on 155mm calibre. This can carry a variety of sub-munitions or a large weight of HE and provides a good destructive effect. It is also the heaviest calibre that can be carried by one man without too much difficulty. Larger calibre guns will no doubt be retained by some nations, but the developing consensus is that rockets can perform tasks, such as depth fire, rather more effectively than such guns.

Range

Although guns do have a longer minimum range than mortars, this is unlikely to be a significant problem since they will usually be deployed several kilometres to the rear of the front line and associated close targets. The maximum range of guns is constantly being increased, 40km being quite possible especially with assisted ammunition, and they are thus becoming comparable with many rocket systems. However, they cannot compete with rockets for really long ranges, and anything further than 50km will almost certainly require a rocket.

Rate of Fire

Modern guns can provide excellent burst fire rates of three rounds in ten seconds, and intense rates of six rounds per minute for three minutes. They can then sustain fire for an hour or more at low rates (two rounds per minute), although this is dependent on barrel heating and hence on the charge being fired. Such rates are noticeably slower than mortars, although the target effect, especially from 155mm guns, is far greater than that from a comparable number of mortars. In comparison with rockets, only a large concentration of guns can hope to match the shock effect of an MLRS but, as stated earlier, the guns will be able to sustain fire for far longer.

ROCKET LAUNCHERS

General Characteristics

The prime difference between a rocket and a mortar or a gun is that the rocket does not exert a significant force or pressure on its launcher as it is fired. The forward thrust is obtained as a reaction to the acceleration of the gases which escape from the open end of the rocket and the launch tube. As a minimum, the launcher only has to support the rocket and point it in the required direction for firing. Consequently, it can be very simple and light. Furthermore, changes to the size or range of the rocket need not have major implications for modification or design of the launcher.

Mobility and Protection

The potential light weight of a rocket launcher is evidently beneficial for mobility. However, high mobility is almost certainly a vital characteristic since rockets are launched with an obvious signature from their gas efflux, and need to move as quickly as possible after firing. Most launchers are self-propelled, either wheeled or tracked, and will have no problem doing this, but even launchers mounted on trailers should not take long to come out of action and move away from the firing point. It is this mobility which provides most of the protection for a rocket system. Some launchers do have light armour, but most are little more than modified trucks.

Ammunition

The low acceleration of a rocket (typically 50–250 G) places few constraints on the design of the warhead to sustain launch forces. The warhead volume can fill the available space without the need for thick walls to the casing, and delicate electronic components can be used in fuzes and sensors for terminally guided munitions. Consequently, large warheads, either of high explosive, improved conventional munitions such as bomblets and minelets, or chemical weapons, can easily be fitted. This provides a rocket system with the ability to deliver a very heavy weight of fire in a short space of time. Conversely, rockets are not well suited to having less destructive warheads such as smoke since, unless they are of small calibre, they would deliver an excessive quantity in one place.

Range

Rockets are generally far superior to mortars and guns in terms of maximum range. For a given size of rocket, range is basically the result of a trade-off between the size of the motor and the warhead volume and weight: the larger

Figure 3.7 Multiple Launch Rocket System (MLRS) Firing

the motor, the longer the range, but the smaller the warhead. Minimum range is a problem for rockets, however, since they only have one charge and this leads to problems of crest clearance as described earlier in this chapter. Furthermore, the low angle of descent at very short range can lead to a poor dispersion pattern of submunitions.

The accuracy and consistency of rockets can be severely affected by crosswinds, thrust misalignment and slight variations in the burning characteristics of the motor. This can be overcome to some extent in modern systems by fitting relatively cheap navigation and guidance systems, although this will reduce either motor or warhead size.

The result of the above characteristics is that rockets are not well suited to close support tasks where accurate fire will be required at relatively short ranges.

Rate of Fire

The rate of fire from a rocket system must be considered in two respects. Firstly, very high burst rates of fire are possible, especially from multiple launchers since all the munitions are loaded and can be fired in a matter of seconds. For example, even the aging Russian BM21 launcher can deliver almost one tonne of high explosive onto a target in 20 seconds, whereas it would take about six AS90s at burst fire rates to do the same. Another useful comparison is that one MLRS delivers 7,728 bomblets onto a target in 50 seconds compared with 14 AS90s firing standard (M483) bomblet shells. Even then, in this example, the AS90 could only achieve two-thirds of the maximum range of an MLRS.

Secondly, however, the time taken to reload and resupply a rocket system will be much longer than that of a gun. The BM21 takes about ten minutes to reload, and the MLRS about three minutes, but this does not allow for the need to move after firing, as discussed above. In practice, MLRS will take at least 15 minutes to fire, move, reload, move and fire again. For sustained operations this should be increased to at least 30 minutes. In comparison, and given an adequate detachment size, a gun or mortar can reload shells or bombs in seconds for a considerable period of time. In terms of resupply, a DROPS vehicle (see Chapter 2) without a trailer can carry 24 MLRS rockets (which might be sufficient for up to two hours) or 170 complete 155mm rounds (which might be sufficient for up to 12 hours). There are two reasons for this: for a given range, more propellant is needed in a rocket motor than for a gun; and the motor casing travels as part of the rocket after launch.

SUMMARY

It should now be evident that mortars, guns and rockets have different characteristics which are in fact complementary. This is particularly true when the requirements of a force capable of flexible operations are considered. Most armies will therefore aim to field a mixture of these weapons, and will tailor the force package for a particular operation according to the circumstances at the time.

At Annex A to this Chapter is a table summarising the preceding paragraphs, comparing the advantages and disadvantages of mortars, guns and rockets.

ANNEX A TO
CHAPTER 3

Comparison of Weapon Platforms

System	Advantages	Disadvantages
Mortars	Very light: high overall mobility	Limited range
	Simple and cheap: good for conscripts	No low angle fire: easy to locate
	Low maintenance	Long time of flight
	Good lethality against unprotected troops	Requirement to 'bed-in': poor initial accuracy
	Good rate of fire	No direct fire capability
	Quick into and out of action	No big advantages over SP guns when mounted under amour
	Easy to dig in and conceal	Very limited against hard targets
	Good guarantee of intimate support	
Guns	Good range coverage	Limited capability against MBTs (but this should improve soon)
	Good accuracy and consistency	Poor strategic mobility (especially SP guns)
	Good sustained fire capability	
	Good weight of fire	Increased weight for greater range
	Good response times	Greater logistic load than mortars
	Fair capability against light armour	Difficult to dig in and concea
	Good tactical mobility (especially SP guns)	Limited guarantee of intimate support
	Direct fire capability	Complex and expensive
Rockets	Long range possible without increase in platform weight	Accuracy and consistency worse than guns
	Very good initial weight of fire: shock effect	High minimum range
	Versatile payload	Significant logistic load
	Good potential for smart sub-munitions: good anti-armour capability	Poor sustained fire capability
		Relatively long response time
		Poor strategic mobility
	Good tactical mobility	No direct fire capability

4

....

Mortars

INTRODUCTION

The main characteristics of mortars compared with guns and rockets have been covered in Chapter 3. In summary, most 'orthodox' mortars:

- have a smooth bore barrel with muzzle loading;
- fire a fin-stabilised bomb with propellant charge attached;
- fire at the high angle (above 800mils) and have no recoil system.

The prime advantages of a mortar are its simplicity, its relatively low weight and hence high mobility, and the fact that given its short range it is likely to remain dedicated to the fire support of its operating unit. These factors should be borne in mind when considering improvements or new systems. For example, taking a typical battalion or battlegroup mortar, an increase in range or calibre will almost certainly lead to an increase in weight of both the mortar tube and its ammunition. This will impose greater loads for the soldiers to carry and may indeed preclude the possibility of manportability. Larger mortars become similar in some respects to light guns, but have several relative disadvantages. Furthermore, a significant increase in range may allow the weapon to fire into areas outside the battalion area of influence; logically it should then be commanded at a higher level, and so its guarantee of support may be removed. On the other hand, troops tend to be more dispersed on modern battlefields and so the need for greater ranges may become more important and outweigh the penalties involved. Other improvements to the complete mortar system, such as fire control systems, are considered in Chapters 2, 3 and 7.

A professional armed force is likely to use artillery for long-range indirect fire. This situation leads to the adoption of light mortars, typically of 50mm calibre, for short ranges and medium mortars, typically of 81mm calibre, which achieve a good balance between manportable weight and an adequate target effect. However, the relative simplicity, reliability and low cost of even heavy mortars (over 100mm calibre) may make them more attractive than guns to conscript armies who have limited training time.

AMMUNITION

Roles

A mortar will generally have three, and possibly four, roles. These are to fire against personnel targets, to provide illumination and smoke, and perhaps to fire against armoured targets.

Bomb Shape and Weight

A typical mortar bomb is fin-stabilised, with a nose fuze and the propellant charge mounted around the tail boom. For stability, the centre of gravity should be well forward of the centre of pressure. This is not necessarily easy to achieve without decreasing lethality or increasing bomb length by an inconvenient amount.

Spin

An unspun fin-stabilised bomb, unless perfectly symmetrical about its longitudinal axis, will not fly true and so will be inaccurate. However, spinning increases air resistance and thus reduces range. Moreover, slight spin can lead to 'spin/yaw resonance' which in turn leads to instability. Nevertheless, current successful practice is to go for low spin and very accurate production techniques.

Fragmentation

Most lethality comes from fragmentation of the body, rather than from the shock wave of the explosive blast. For optimum fragmentation, the body must be made of special materials such as spheroidal graphite cast iron which produces a high proportion of fragments of ideal weight (around 1 gm) travelling at high velocity (around 1,500m/s). Particles much larger than this will decelerate quickly, limiting the lethal radius of the bomb, while much smaller particles will have insufficient energy to cause injuries to lightly protected targets.

Anti-Armour Bombs

Some attempts have been made to design pre-fragmented bombs but these are most unlikely to have enough energy to penetrate modern lightly armoured vehicles. A more promising solution is to use terminal guidance and a HEAT warhead to attack the top of armoured vehicles, sometimes referred to as Mortar Anti-Tank (MORAT). This is the concept for weapons such as the British Aerospace

Merlin, the Bofors Strix and the Diehl Bussard which have radar or infra-red seekers and which have been under trial for several years. There are size and weight penalties so range is reduced and fewer bombs can be carried. Such bombs are likely to cost about 50 times as much as HE bombs, so their cost-effectiveness compared to other anti-armour systems must be considered. However, MORAT would provide a useful additional anti-tank capability for dismounted forces such as Marines and Parachutists and could be considered either as a complement or an alternative to a direct fire guided weapon.

Bomb Trajectory

At the top of its trajectory, the apogee, a bomb has no vertical velocity and when fired at high elevation it also has very little horizontal velocity. Thus it is likely to be very susceptible to meteorological conditions and so precise fire can be very difficult to achieve.

Charge Systems

It can be shown that for practical purposes the minimum range of a single, primary charge mortar is about one-third of the maximum range. This may be acceptable for platoon mortars, but for most purposes it is far too restrictive. Consequently secondary charge systems are used, with normally at least three and up to fourteen increments available. This is an unavoidable complication.

Extended Range Bombs

Various methods of extending the range of bombs have been tried. A discarding sabot bomb has flown to 20km but it was inaccurate and had a very small

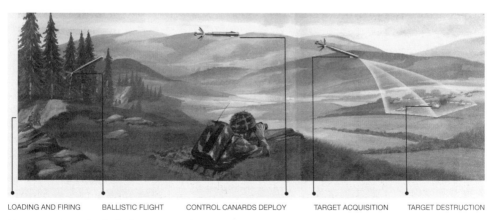

LOADING AND FIRING   BALLISTIC FLIGHT   CONTROL CANARDS DEPLOY   TARGET ACQUISITION   TARGET DESTRUCTION

Figure 4.1 Typical Flight Pattern for a MORAT Bomb

payload. Rocket assistance has been used, with ranges of 9km for a 120mm bomb but with similar penalties.

BASEPLATES

Requirements

A baseplate supports the breech end of the barrel and it transmits the firing forces into the ground which absorbs them and thus provides the recoil system for a mortar. Consequently a baseplate must provide firm and stable support, prevent excessive rebound, allow good traverse of the firing arc (ideally 360 degrees or 6,400 mils) and be robust yet light enough and convenient to carry. It must also be easy to remove from soft ground, a design feature which can be difficult to meet.

Ground

The soil bearing strength of surfaces on which a baseplate may have to sit can vary significantly from 200 KN/m^2 for soft clay to 30,000 KN/m^2 for hard rock, a difference of a factor of 150. The strength of softer ground will improve with compaction as the mortar is fired and beds in. Given such variations, the design of a baseplate to suit all conditions may well be impossible.

These problems may be overcome by extensive preparation of the ground from which the mortar is to be fired, by digging and possibly laying a hard surface. However, this will take time and effectively removes one of the prime advantages of a mortar – its mobility. Unless its operators are constrained by factors outside their control to remain in one position, they will almost certainly wish to move regularly, since mortars can easily be located by radar or bomb crater analysis, and they will then be liable to counter-fire.

Bedding In

A technique generally used to provide a more stable platform for the baseplate, and hence the mortar, is termed 'bedding-in'. This is achieved by firing two rounds, usually at high elevation and high charge, to settle the baseplate into the ground. It should improve the accuracy and consistency of subsequent rounds. However, continued firing is still likely to sink the baseplate a little further except in very hard ground, and contact with rocks or other obstructions may occur. This may cause instability through the baseplate pivoting about the obstruction, and it also leads to the requirement for the plate to be strong enough to withstand such local forces. Bedding-in does have the disadvantages of wastage of ammunition and possible early compromise of the mortar location. It can also be difficult to achieve in some surfaces, although the use of aids such as the Raschen Bag System, developed for the 81mm mortar, can be beneficial.

Baseplate Design

When a mortar fires there are both vertical and horizontal components of the recoil force. At an elevation of 800 mils these will be equal, but the horizontal component will obviously decrease as the elevation is increased. Nevertheless, even at 1,000 mils the horizontal force will be significant and is likely to lead to rearward movement of the mortar and hence instability and inaccuracy. A baseplate therefore needs teeth or a spike to ensure that it bites into the surface and can take the horizontal component of recoil force without excessive movement. Perversely, while hard ground is better for preventing sinkage and thus maintaining stability, the teeth or spike will find it more difficult to bite into such ground and hence provide lateral stability. Consequently, preparation to absorb the horizontal force is normally required, and unless the mortar has been dug in this might mean the use of sandbags.

Some baseplates are designed to slope at an angle on flat ground, usually with shorter teeth or spikes at the front and longer ones at the rear. This tends to transmit the recoil force at approximately right angles to the plate and parallel to the spikes, providing a more stable support. Such a design precludes all-round traverse and so is less flexible than a symmetrical baseplate. However, after protracted firing in one direction, the teeth on the latter design are likely to leave holes behind them and so the plate will probably need to be repositioned anyway if a large switch in firing direction is needed.

If a mortar is fired below 800 mils the horizontal component of recoil increases as the elevation decreases. It becomes more difficult to absorb the force adequately and so firing in the low angle is usually avoided.

The shape, area and configuration of teeth or spikes of a baseplate all depend on the recoil force that it has to transmit and the nature of the ground on which it is expected to be used. Many baseplates have holes in them both to prevent air being trapped which would provide an elastic cushion, and also to reduce suction thus facilitating their extraction.

Although barrels can be fixed rigidly to the baseplate, this usually only applies to lighter mortars. Such mortars are simpler and quicker to emplace, but traverse can be impeded. Larger barrels would almost certainly be too heavy to carry with their baseplate so they are separate components. Hence medium and heavy mortar barrels invariably have a ball joint at their end which fits into a socket on the baseplate. The joint usually has two flat sides which effectively lock the ball into the socket once fitted and rotated through

Figure 4.2 Mortar with Angled Baseplate

90 degrees. The area of the baseplate under the socket must be strengthened in some way since this has to absorb the greatest recoil force and transmit it across the plate without shearing.

Some baseplates have been designed in sections so that only sufficient parts need to be used according to the soil conditions. Although superficially an attractive concept, it has its penalties. The sections must have strong joints to transmit the recoil forces, which will increase weight and may make disassembly difficult due to distortion. Furthermore, unless the soil conditions are very predictable then the full range of sections will need to be carried and this will cancel the main advantage of such a system.

Materials

The baseplate must be ductile to allow it to absorb recoil forces without fracture when it is still proud of the ground surface. Combining this factor with the need for strength means that steel has been the most common material for baseplates. More recently magnesium and aluminium alloys have also been used in manufacture. More exotic materials with very high strength to weight ratios and adequate ductility could be used but they are still very expensive both to supply and to fabricate, and are not yet cost-effective.

BARRELS

Requirements

The barrel must be long enough both to accelerate the bomb to the muzzle velocity required for maximum range and also to provide reasonable accuracy. Conversely for manportable equipment the barrel should be as short as possible to save weight and make it as easy as possible to carry and to load. If long range and manportability are both important the barrel could be designed in two parts which are screwed together, such as the Finnish Tampella 81mm. In addition to more obvious requirements such as safety and robustness, a barrel must be able to dissipate sufficient heat at the specified rates of sustained fire, transmit firing forces to the mounting, and include a means of initiating the bomb's propellant charge.

Barrel Strength

Because mortars have much shorter ranges than guns of similar calibre their maximum barrel pressures are much lower than those of a gun. Typical values of maximum pressure are 30 MPa for a light mortar and 100 MPa for a medium mortar, compared to 300 MPa for a light gun. At the muzzle the comparative figures might be 15 and 70 MPa. In practice barrel strength is often governed more by rough handling requirements than by firing stresses. Using high strength steels, barrels can be reasonably light and current weights are considered acceptable. Although any decrease in weight would be useful, it must be remembered that most of the weight of a complete mortar system is due to the ammunition, so the return on using expensive light alloys will not be significant other than perhaps for special forces.

Strength must be maintained at high temperature, and the British 81mm mortar is designed not to exceed 550°C, which it will reach after firing 15 bombs per minute (or rounds per minute) for 15 minutes. It is worth noting that even in war, high rates of fire are rarely maintained, the highest known in British experience being three rpm for one hour and 18 rpm for five minutes (both in Italy in 1944). The 81mm is probably stronger than it needs to be, although its over-design has given it stretch potential and helped it to meet additional demands for foreign sales.

Barrel Cooling

Barrel cooling is achieved through convection and radiation, the latter being predominant above about 300°C. Provided temperatures can be kept below 350°C finned barrel design should not be necessary. For mortars mounted inside an armoured vehicle barrel, heating can become a problem for crew comfort, especially since there will be little air movement to assist convection, and this may be a limiting factor on rates of fire.

Figure 4.3 Cross-section of a UK 81mm Mortar Barrel

Note: The fins are only not required around the top section of the barrel, which is smooth.

Obturation and Windage

The inherent requirement of having a bomb with a loose enough fit to be easily loaded, yet needing to provide a tight gas seal on firing, leads to several design problems. The term windage refers to the difference between the diameter of the bore and the diameter of the mortar bomb. If windage is insufficient, air in the barrel will be unable to escape quickly enough as the bomb slides down the barrel and the resulting air cushion will slow the bomb down as it falls or could even stop it. If there is a fixed firing pin the resulting impact velocity may be insufficient to ignite the charge. Even if it does fire, a slow rate of fall may reduce the rate of fire unacceptably. However, windage must not be so great that it allows the escape of too much gas around the bomb after firing, which would decrease range and might increase wear and inaccuracy.

The windage dimension must also allow for the change in barrel diameter caused by heating and wear. The former decreases windage and the latter increases it. The minimum windage for an 81mm mortar is of the order of 0.6mm, and a reduction in windage of 0.5mm will occur at temperatures over 500°C. Consequently if dirt or fouling from propellant residue is present in the bore this can cause problems.

Despite the need for windage, it is obviously necessary to provide forward obturation around the bomb when it is fired. The simplest approach, commonly used in the past, is to provide a series of lateral grooves around the maximum diameter of the bomb so that they provide a form of turbulent baffle as the gases try to move past them. However, when the bomb is in flight this turbulence will still occur in the air around it, affecting range and accuracy. Furthermore, this technique cannot allow for the variations in windage described above. Probably the best, and simplest, solution is to use a split-ring of plastic with its unextended diameter just less than the bomb's body, seated

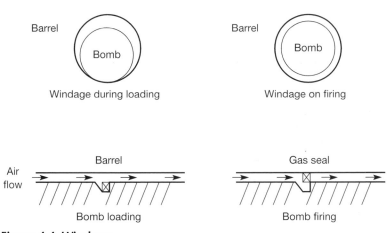

Figure 4.4 Windage

in a groove. On firing, the propellant pressure expands the scarfed joint so that seals are formed between the wall, the ring and the bomb.

An alternative approach has been to use an air valve near the base of the barrel. This is open as the bomb slides down but is pushed closed by the tail fins as they pass. Gas pressure then keeps the valve closed until the bomb leaves the barrel and air pressure is equalised. This approach is not without its problems since the clearance between the bomb and bore must be adequate to facilitate loading yet it will vary with barrel temperature and thus cause inconsistencies in bore pressures.

Wear

Wear in mortar barrels tends to be low. Abrasive wear is caused by the bombs' tail fins touching the bore. Erosive wear is caused by the action of the gases at high pressure, temperature and velocity, particularly at any point of leakage around the obturation of the bomb, but it is rarely significant because gas pressure is relatively low compared to that of a gun. Abrasive wear can be reduced by careful machining of the bore to give a very smooth finish. Chrome plating has been used on some mortars, but it is an expensive process and may well not be worth the cost in terms of extending barrel life.

Moisture and Fouling

Because a mortar barrel is invariably elevated to high angles of elevation there is a strong likelihood that rain will collect in it even if a muzzle cover is used between fire missions. Although this should not affect ignition, moisture is likely to affect the rate at which propellant burns and thus compromise bore pressure and muzzle velocity, leading to inconsistency.

Fouling in the bore can be caused by dirt and grease on the ammunition, traces of lubricants, particles of the obturating ring, and any residue from unconsumed charge. The combined effect of these will produce a sticky coating on the bore which, if allowed to build up, will decrease windage and reduce the rate of fire. Careful handling of ammunition can reduce this problem, but swabbing out of the bore will be necessary at regular intervals as a precaution.

Firing Mechanisms

Most medium mortars have a fixed firing pin, which avoids complexity of design and maintenance. The pin will be removable in order to allow cleaning and inspection for damage. However, a firing mechanism may be required when the mortar is hand-held (in order to check the lay after loading) and when bomb momentum is low (e.g. with light bombs or if the mortar can be fired at a low angle, as in a gun-mortar). A firing mechanism can assist with a rapid response to a call for fire from a pre-arranged target since the mortar can be loaded and aimed beforehand, leaving only the trigger to be operated. Some Russian mortars have a fixed pin which can be interrupted by an optional firing mechanism when required.

BARREL SUPPORTS

Other than for light mortars, where a man's hand can be adequate, a mechanical device is needed to support the barrel. Bipods are the most common form of support, but monopods and tripods have been used.

A bipod must support the barrel at all required angles, allow for fine adjustment of elevation and quick switches of line, be simple to erect and operate even on irregular ground, withstand firing stresses, and be easy to handle and carry. It will probably have to support a sight and cushion it from the firing shock. It may also have to allow independent movement of the barrel during firing in order to avoid large forces being transmitted through the bipod itself.

In order to meet all these requirements, a bipod consists of structural members and gears, and possibly shock absorbers as well. The two legs are often braced by a cross member for extra strength, and their feet should have plates in order to prevent the legs sinking too far into the ground. The gears allow the barrel orientation to be finely adjusted, but their traverse action will be limited so it should always be possible to move the legs easily to accommodate large changes in bearing. The bipod may incorporate a cross-levelling device in order to maintain the sight in a vertical axis on uneven ground. The shock absorbers usually consist of one or more cylinders containing springs, although hydraulic systems have been used in heavy mortars.

Obviously a bipod should be as light as possible in order to assist manportability. This is relatively easy to achieve since it does not have to absorb the main firing stresses so it only needs to be strong enough to support the barrel and light alloys can therefore be used. Durability to avoid damage from rough handling is also an important consideration, and to ease carriage the bipod is usually designed to be folded when not in use. Despite all this, the bipod is often the most expensive sub-assembly of the mortar since many components for traverse, elevation and levelling have to be machined accurately.

SIGHTS

For light mortars with short range, where the target can usually be seen, only a simple sighting system such as a line on the barrel may be required. However,

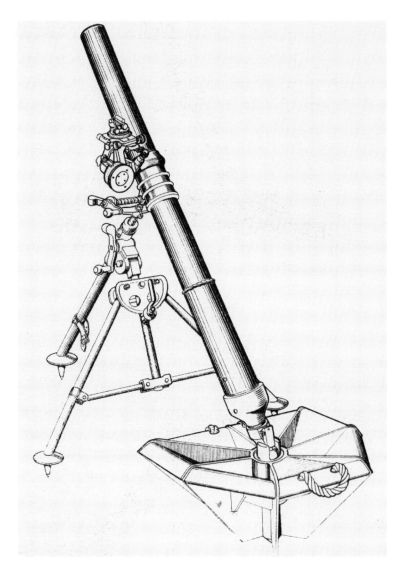

Figure 4.5 British 4.2 inch Mortar with Tripod

once the mortar becomes a true indirect fire weapon platform it will require a more sophisticated sight which will need to be robust enough to withstand the accelerations of firing and recoil. A sight is normally the most fragile component of a mortar and will be removed from its mount during movement.

Sights incorporate fine and coarse scales for both bearing and elevation, and some form of cross level. Although some sights have an elevation scale which is marked off with range information, mortars using several charges must have an elevation angle set onto the sight, this being calculated from range tables or by a small ballistic computer.

Figure 4.6 American 4.2 inch Mortar with Monopod

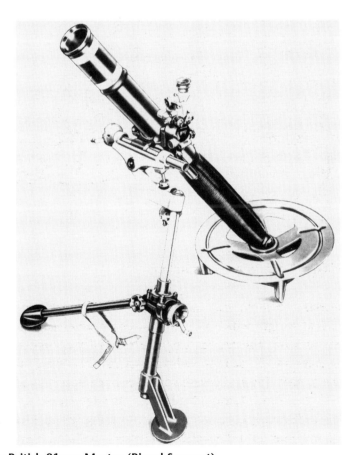

Figure 4.7 The British 81mm Mortar (Bipod Support)

RIFLED MORTARS

The accuracy of a mortar can be improved by using rifling to impart spin to the bomb since, as discussed in Chapter 3, this improves stability. This is particularly significant at transonic and supersonic velocities where the instability of airflow and shock waves around the fins of a bomb can cause large inaccuracies and inconsistencies. Consequently mortars designed to achieve long ranges, and thus requiring a high muzzle velocity, may be rifled. The Hotchkiss-Brandt 120mm rifled mortar is a good example of such a system.

Rifling on a muzzle loaded mortar naturally tends to complicate the design of the bomb. Usually, the driving band of the bomb is pre-engraved with slots to match the rifling. The bomb then has to be aligned carefully with the rifling before it is loaded, and even then its fall down the barrel may be slow, leading to the need for a firing mechanism. Consequently the rate of fire of a rifled mortar is likely to be less than for a smooth-bored one. An alternative approach has been to make the driving band diameter less than the calibre of the barrel and then to expand the band by means of a small charge on firing. This is, however, both complicated and prone to unreliability and has not been used for many years.

Breech Loading

Breech loading can overcome some of the problems associated with rifled mortars, and indeed many of the mortars designed in the 20th century have been breech loaders. They tend to have disadvantages compared to muzzle loaders of similar calibre in that access to the breech can be difficult, the breech will make them heavier and the rate of fire is likely to be less due to the loading action and the use of a firing mechanism. Nevertheless, they do have some advantages if the mortar is to be mounted in a vehicle.

MORTARS IN VEHICLES

A vehicle-mounted mortar has obvious advantages for mechanised forces because of the speed it can go into action and, most important, it provides an immediately available large supply of ammunition. Furthermore, bedding-in is not required. However, a vehicle is expensive to acquire and maintain, and it cannot reach places only accessible to men on foot. Its strategic mobility and, to some extent, its tactical mobility will therefore be less than for a man-portable mortar. Moreover, unless the mortar is mounted in a turret, the vehicle only provides limited crew protection, and virtually none against air-burst attack. For reasons of cost it is most unlikely that a new vehicle will be designed specifically to carry a mortar. It is much more likely that an existing vehicle will be converted. There are two ways of doing this: the hybrid mortar and the turreted gun-mortar.

Hybrid Mortars

Firstly, an armoured personnel carrier can have its crew compartment adapted to carry an existing ground-mounted mortar. Problems in adapting the vehicle can then occur; for example, the British FV432 requires a raised turntable to allow the 81mm mortar to be fired at all elevations and orientations and to avoid dangerous muzzle pressures developing inside the crew compartment. This turntable is sprung in order to divert some of the firing loads from the torsion bar suspension.

The Tampella 120mm mortar, mounted in the US Army M113, cannot achieve a 360° traverse without movement of the vehicle on its tracks. Furthermore, the vehicle suspension system may have to be strengthened or provided with a lock out, in order to absorb firing stresses. Nevertheless, this concept is relatively cheap since there is only a limited conversion to be done and often older APCs, which have been replaced in their original role by a newer type, can be used. A further advantage is that the mortar can usually be dismounted if necessary for the ground role. This provides extra flexibility for the force, will aid ammunition compatibility and reduce training requirements for a mixed force which should be able to use only one type of mortar for all tasks.

Figure 4.8 British 81mm Mortar in the FV 432

Figure 4.9 French AMX 13 120mm Mortar Carrier

Note: This is an example of a hybrid mortar. Note also the baseplate fitted to the front of the vehicle for use in the ground role.

Turreted or Gun-Mortars

A turret mounted, breech loading weapon platform which fires a mortar bomb is often termed a 'gun-mortar'. Such systems have been designed by, amongst others, Thomson-Brandt of France (60mm and 81mm) and the Russians who have produced the 2S9, 2S23 and 2S31 (all 120mm), the last being mounted on a BMD chassis with autonomous navigation and computation systems. More recently, Royal Ordnance in Britain has developed a 120mm mortar mounted in a Delco turret from the USA which can be fitted to a wide range of light armoured vehicles such as the Piranha and the M113.

In addition to the advantages of a hybrid mortar, a gun-mortar could use a heavier barrel and higher charges to extend range. It need not fire in the high angle, so its accuracy could be less affected by meteorological conditions, and its configuration does not take up so much space inside the vehicle thus leaving more room for ammunition stowage. Furthermore, the fact that most of these systems can be fired in the low angle means that they have a direct fire capability, although this is unlikely to be very accurate above about 1,000m.

However, while a gun-mortar is not dissimilar to an SP gun, it will almost certainly have less range and be less accurate, its rate of fire will be constrained by its breech-loading action, and it may not be significantly cheaper. Moreover, most guns, especially SP types, are being designed at about 155mm calibre to achieve a useful target effect in armoured warfare. Consequently even a 120 mm gun-mortar could well have the disadvantages of both mortars and small calibre guns without many of the advantages of either. Nevertheless,

Figure 4.10 Royal Ordnance 120mm Turreted Mortar

they continue to be developed and some countries may perceive that their relative simplicity and suitability for mechanised infantry may make them more attractive than light SP guns.

TOWED MORTARS

An alternative to the vehicle-mounted mortar is the towed mortar, where the assembly is mounted on a trailer. This configuration can be relatively cheap to produce since there is no need for a specialist vehicle conversion. However, its cross-country mobility is unlikely to be as good as vehicles in a mechanised force, so it is only suitable for deployment with forces equipped with light vehicles.

Figure 4.11 Finnish Tampella 120mm Towed Mortar

LIGHT MORTARS

A light mortar is often carried by the infantry at platoon or section level and on patrols, to provide fire support at almost immediate notice. In many cases this support is needed at short ranges – 50 to 150m – when it becomes almost direct fire.

Increasingly, however, light mortars are being used at ranges of up to 2,000m to provide protective fire, smoke and illumination across dispersed groups, especially when other indirect fire resources are not available. They typically have calibres of between 50 and 65mm. They can be very simple, with a small baseplate often permanently fixed to the barrel, and very light, weighing perhaps 5 to 7kg, although once a sight, bipod and more substantial baseplate are included this rises to about 14kg. Bombs weigh between 1kg for a 51mm mortar and 4.3kg for a 60mm mortar. Extended range ammunition is also available for some systems which, when used in conjunction with a longer barrel, can give ranges of up to 6,000m. They have a limited target effect in comparison with medium mortars and light artillery, but their manportability, versatility and immediate readiness at a low level can nevertheless make them valuable as infantry close with the enemy.

Figure 4.12 Hand-held Light Mortar being Loaded

IMPROVISED MORTARS

Most light weapons have been seen in improvised form, and the mortar is no exception. For example, its simplicity and ease of manufacture from materials which are readily available make it suitable for construction by terrorist forces. Most recently the development of mortars for use by the Provisional Irish Republican Army in Northern Ireland has become quite sophisticated. These devices are normally made by welding steel tubes to a metal plate at an elevation corresponding to the range from a predetermined firing position, and mounting this construction in a van or lorry. The bombs are pre-loaded and the vehicle is driven into position and then fired remotely. The latter action is necessary because of the unreliability of the barrels and bombs: in several cases the whole vehicle has exploded during the firing sequence. Nevertheless, such devices show what can be achieved with very simple technology.

SUMMARY

Although heavy mortars are used by the artillery of some armies, the mortar is primarily an infantry weapon and the infantry value its simplicity. This chap-

Figure 4.13 Hand-held Light Mortar being Carried

ter has described many ways in which the capability of basic mortars can be increased, but in most cases such developments have associated disadvantages or at least present complications. Any attempt to complicate a mortar should be considered very carefully since in battle, particularly with infantry operations, simplicity can have tremendous value.

5

......

Artillery Guns

INTRODUCTION

The two main groups of components of a gun are the carriage or mounting, and the ordnance. The carriage or mounting supports the ordnance, provides stability for the gun on firing, includes the arrangements for pointing the gun in the required direction and in some cases provides a means of transporting the ordnance. The ordnance contains the pressure of the burning charge in such a way that the energy produced is transmitted safely and predictably to the projectile. It also includes a means of imparting direction and stability to the projectile.

SECTION 1 – ORDNANCE

The main components of the ordnance are the barrel and its attachments, the breech, and the firing mechanism.

The Barrel

Sequence of Events on Firing
The study of the motion of projectiles inside a gun is termed Internal Ballistics, which also includes the study of the ballistic properties of propellants. This is studied in detail in Volume I of this Series[1], but the key aspects are considered here since they are the prime determinants of barrel design.

When a gun fires, the burning charge produces gases at very high pressures which accelerate the projectile through the bore until it leaves the muzzle. The velocity with which it leaves the muzzle is the basic determinant of the range which the projectile will achieve, although many other factors such as the weight and shape of the projectile and the atmospheric conditions will also influence the range. In order to achieve maximum accuracy and consistency it is obviously necessary to ensure that the muzzle velocity required is produced in a predictable manner and that variations from round to round are as small as possible. It is also highly desirable that the process of achieving the muzzle velocity is as efficient as possible: this will minimise the quantity of charge to be transported and reduce barrel heating. A typical distribution of the energy from the ignited charge in a 155mm gun is given in Figure 5.1.

It can be seen that the process is not particularly efficient, considerable quantities of energy being lost in heat and in accelerating the propellant gases up the bore. Thermal efficiency and repeatability are therefore major considerations for the gun designer.

Once the propellant is ignited, it begins to burn in the space between the forward and rearward obturation. Obturation is the term used to describe the means of sealing the propellant gases in the barrel. Forward obturation is provided by the base of the shell and the driving band which engages in the rifling of the barrel. Rearward obturation is discussed in detail later, but is either provided by a cartridge case or by a seal in the breech mechanism. The rate of burning of the propellant increases faster than the rate of increase in gas pressure. Eventually, the pressure reaches a value at which the shell begins to move up the bore. As the projectile moves, the space available for the gases increases and thus the rate of increase in pressure will tend to decrease. The extent to which this rate decreases depends upon whether the propellant burns progressively, neutrally or regressively. The surface area of a progressive propellant increases as burning continues, that of a neutral propellant stays constant, and the surface area of a regressive propellant reduces. The gun designer can therefore control to some extent the variation of pressure by the shape and size of propellant he uses.

Maximum pressure is reached when the pressure increase from burning propellant equals the pressure loss due to the increasing space behind the shell. Thereafter the pressure begins to drop. However, the projectile continues to accelerate because the gas is still doing work on its base. For this reason also

Projectile Kinetic Energy	35%
Propellant Gas Internal Energy	40%
Heat Transfer to Barrel	20%
Friction Losses	3%
Spin	2%

Figure 5.1 Typical Distribution of Propellant Energy

the projectile will continue to accelerate even after the charge is all burnt, until it emerges from the muzzle. Figure 5.2 shows the relationship between pressure, velocity and distance travelled down the bore for a typical gun. It should be noted however that there is a pressure gradient within the gases; i.e. the pressure at the base of the projectile is greater than that at the face of the breech (or the rear of the cartridge case).

Figure 5.2 indicates that there is still a significant pressure in the barrel at projectile exit, and that therefore some more of the energy from the propellant could be used by lengthening the barrel. However, it should be noted from the velocity/space curve that the velocity is not greatly increasing near the muzzle, so that simply lengthening the barrel will only have a limited effect on muzzle velocity. A greater advantage can be gained from also changing the propellant so that the 'all-burnt' position is further down the (longer) barrel, allowing more work to be done on the projectile. Whether or not this is done, if very long range is required the longest practicable barrel may well be used.

The 'all burnt' position, also shown on Figure 5.2, is a very significant factor in gun design. If 'all burnt' is near the breech, this will provide better consistency in muzzle velocity and lower muzzle pressure, leading to higher thermal efficiency and hence a smaller charge. However, it will also mean that the peak barrel pressure is high, which will make gun design more difficult. If 'all burnt' is nearer the muzzle, consistency will be less but piezometric efficiency will be higher which will make gun design easier. Note also that if the shell has left the barrel before the charge is all burnt there is a danger that the breech could be opened before

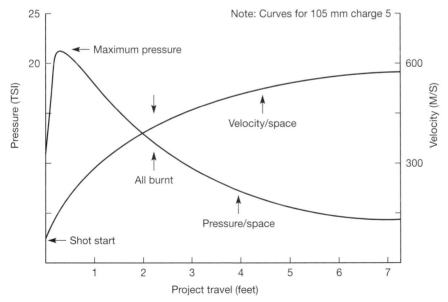

Figure 5.2 Pressure/Velocity/Space Curves

all the propellant has been consumed, thus posing a danger to the gun detachment. Even if it is within the barrel but still too far forward there is a likelihood of an obvious muzzle flash which will assist hostile detection.

Barrel Characteristics

The main characteristics of a barrel are that it must have a long life, strength, stiffness and an appropriate centre of gravity.

Barrel Life

The service life of a barrel needs to be as long as practicable both in order to minimise barrel changes, especially in operational conditions, and for cost reasons. The life can be extended by various means such as special bore surface finishes, barrel cooling, and the use of additives to create cool burning propellants. However, such techniques are likely to be expensive and it may be more economic to provide simpler and cheaper replacement barrels. Decisions will be based on operational requirements and on a cost benefit analysis.

Stresses on Barrels

Figure 5.3 shows the five different stresses which act on gun barrels. Bending (or Girder) stress is due simply to the weight of the barrel and leads to muzzle droop. On firing, gas pressure in the bore imposes a radial stress outwards through the walls of the barrel. The pressure also produces circumferential stress as the barrel tries to expand. The movement of the projectile up the bore produces three further stresses. The first is a localised longitudinal stress due to the difference in pressure between the front and rear of the driving band and this tends to stretch the section of the barrel around the driving band as the projectile moves along. The second is a torsional stress which is a reaction to the force generated as the projectile spins with the rifling. The third is a further bending effect as the barrel tries to straighten as the projectile passes up it.

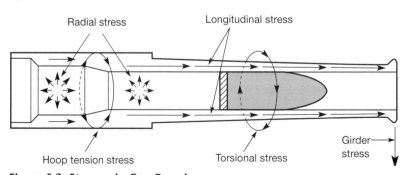

Figure 5.3 Stresses in Gun Barrels

Strength and Stiffness

The strength of the barrel must obviously be adequate to withstand the stresses that are created on firing, together with a margin for safety. The barrel must also be stiff enough not to bend too much due to bending stress and to assist this the barrel thickness is progressively reduced as much as possible towards the muzzle. Adequate barrel strength is achieved by using steel alloys, pre-stressing and design. The required barrel mass is mainly determined by considerations of strength at the breech end and stiffness at the barrel end, and to some extent by the necessary stability of the equipment on firing (as discussed later in this chapter).

Centre of Gravity

The barrel is supported by the cradle which has trunnions that allow these two components to be elevated and depressed in a vertical arc. Such movement would obviously be easiest if the trunnions were at the centre of gravity of the barrel, which would typically be about a third of its total length forward from the breech. However, this positioning would require the trunnions to be high in order to allow the barrel to be elevated to a high angle, which would make the whole gun a tall construction, difficult to conceal, and would also tend to decrease stability. Hence the barrel is normally supported as far back towards the breech as possible, leading to it being muzzle heavy, and consequently balancing gears are required. However, rear trunnions are advantageous in two respects: they tend to allow both more space for recoil and enable easier ammunition handling, since the vertical movement of the breech is less.

BARREL CONSTRUCTION

Wire Wound Barrels

A method of constructing barrels by winding steel wire or ribbon tightly around an inner liner as far forward from the breech as necessary to withstand firing stresses was in use until the early part of the 20th Century. It provided a relatively easy method of pre-stressing the barrel to resist radial, circumferential and torsional stresses, and helped to localise failures, unlike a crack in solid steel which could grow with use. However, it provided very little resistance to longitudinal stress and, in particular, to bending stress. Consequently a metal tube had to be shrunk over the wire to provide greater stiffness, and this complicated the fabrication. Better methods of pre-stressing barrels made this construction method obsolete.

Built-up Barrels

Barrels have been constructed by fitting one or more tubes inside each other. Before assembly the outer tube has a slightly smaller diameter than the inner tube but it is heated and the cold inner tube is then fitted inside it. On cooling, the adjoining surfaces of the two tubes are compressed and this imposes a compressive stress in the inner tube and a tensile stress in the outer tube. The effect is thus to produce a barrel which can withstand a greater bore pressure than an unstressed barrel of the same thickness and monolithic form. This method of construction still has the advantage of relatively easy fabrication for barrels of very large diameter, but since such large guns are rarely built now, it is unlikely to be used often.

Loose Barrels and Loose Liners

Rather than heating up the outer tube of a built-up barrel, it can be slipped on cold, providing a relatively tight fit and increasing barrel strength. There is no pre-stressing so the strengthening effect is not as great as for a built-up barrel, but this construction method does have two advantages. Firstly, it allows the replacement of the inner tube once wear has become too great. Secondly, it allows the barrel to be split into lighter loads for carriage, perhaps by animals. If only part of the length of the barrel has an outer tube then this is a loose barrelled gun; whereas, if the complete barrel has an outer tube this is termed a loose liner. Some versions of the 25pdr, in service with the Royal Artillery throughout the Second World War and used for training until the 1980s, had a loose barrel.

Composite Barrels

A variation of the loose barrel concept is to construct the inner tube of the barrel from several segments made of different grades of steel, the grade of each being determined by the maximum bore pressure at each section of the barrel. The advantage is that a section, rather than the complete inner tube, can be replaced once it becomes too worn. However, such a method requires a complicated manufacturing process, including accurate alignment of the rifling lands and the maintenance of a good gas seal between adjacent segments. Consequently this method of construction has also been replaced by the monobloc form.

Monobloc Barrels

The monobloc form of construction produces a barrel by forging from a single steel billet. This has now become the standard method of production, largely due to the availability of advanced high strength steel alloys and of heavy machine tools with computer control, leading to easier fabrication. Barrels in excess of 10 metres length can now be forged in a few hours of actual working time, although the forging will often need to be heated more than once to complete the work so the total time taken can be up to a day. Furthermore, once forged a considerable amount of heat treatment is used both before and after drilling the bore in order to achieve maximum strength.

For a given grade of steel and bore calibre there is a point where making the barrel wall thicker does not increase barrel strength. This is because if the wall is thick enough the inner layers reach their tensile limit before the outside of the barrel is under any significant stress at all; the outer layers would therefore contribute little to radial or circumferential stress resistance. Therefore to resist higher bore pressures either a steel with higher tensile strength must be used, or the barrel must be pre-stressed.

AutoFrettage

The autofrettage technique was probably invented by the French around the beginning of the 20th Century, and the first autofrettaged gun was a French 140mm produced in 1913. A monobloc barrel whose internal diameter is initially slightly less than the desired calibre is first forged and machined. Then a high pressure is applied inside the barrel either through a hydraulic fluid or by ramming a swage through it. This creates stresses throughout the barrel wall which are greatest adjacent to the bore and least on the outside. The stresses are sufficient to expand the metal closest to the bore beyond its elastic limit so that it is permanently stretched, but are not so great that the outer metal reaches this limit. When the pressure is removed, the outer metal attempts to return to its original dimension but cannot completely do so because the inner metal has expanded. Thus the latter remains compressed. The inner metal is then heat treated to raise its elastic limit. Consequently, when the gun is fired the expansion pressure initially has to overcome the static compression and so the net maximum expansive stresses are lower than they would be in a barrel of similar dimensions which had not been autofrettaged.

The process has several advantages. Firstly, cheaper and lower grade steel could be used in the barrel. Secondly, for a given grade of steel the barrel walls can be thinner, lighter and therefore cheaper (although the cost of the autofrettage process must be taken into account). For example, an autofrettaged 155mm gun might have a maximum external barrel diameter of perhaps 200mm, compared to about 260mm for a non-autofrettaged barrel. Thirdly, the compression tends to close any small cracks in the surface of the bore, which will increase the fatigue life of the barrel by as much as 200%.

Hydraulic Autofrettage
Hydraulic autofrettage is effected by pressurising a fluid, such as a mixture of glycerine and water, inside the bore of the barrel. An example of a type of rig used in the United States is shown in Figure 5.4.

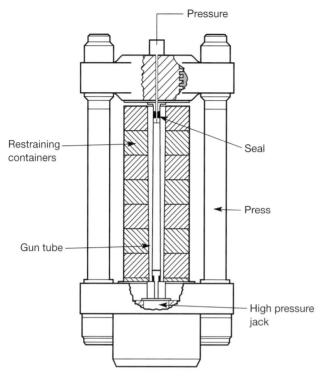

Pressure

Restraining
containers

Seal

Press

Gun tube

High pressure
jack

Figure 5.4 Hydraulic Autofrettage Rig

Since modern high strength steels have very high elastic limits, this can lead to considerable problems in sealing the rig. Furthermore, in order to save weight, a barrel is usually thicker at the breech end than at the muzzle and the difference in wall thickness during autofrettage would lead to different amounts of pre-stressing along the length of the barrel. Thus the barrel must first be constructed and pre-stressed with a constant wall thickness and a subsequent machining process is then required.

Swage Autofrettage

An alternative method of autofrettage is to use a hydraulic press ram to force an oversize swage or mandrel through the bore of the barrel, as shown in Figure 5.5. The pressure which overstrains the inner wall is a function of the grade of steel used in the barrel, the wall thickness, the difference between the initial size of the bore and the swage, and the contact area between the bore and the swage. The advantages of this method over direct hydraulics are that the ram pressure can be less to achieve the same level of pre-stressing, and that if necessary only part of the length of the barrel need be stressed.

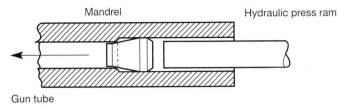

Figure 5.5 Swage Autofrettage

Rifling

Artillery guns are almost invariably rifled. Rifling is engraved into the bore and can have a constant twist or it can be progressive, in which case its angle relative to the bore centreline increases closer to the muzzle. The raised surfaces of the rifling inside the bore of the barrel are called lands. The engagement of the relatively soft driving band on the projectile into the lands allows the rifling to impart spin to the projectile in order to provide it with stability in flight. Progressive rifling reduces the force between the driving band and the lands around the point of maximum gas pressure, yet imparts the desired rate of spin at shot exit. This theoretically allows shorter barrels to be used without degrading projectile stability, while maintaining a shear force on the driving band throughout its movement down the bore. A barrel with constant rifling twist gives a higher initial shear force but this then reduces to a very small amount. Constant twist rifling is easier to manufacture and is normally used in modern guns, although it can lead to a significant torque reaction at the trunnions which needs to be allowed for in design.

The depth of the rifling grooves is a compromise between two factors. Deep grooves improve the guidance of the projectile through the bore and reduce the sensitivity of the barrel to wear. Conversely, shallow grooves allow easier engagement of the driving band in the rifling and produce less air resistance, and hence drag, once the projectile is in flight.

Barrel Wear

Wear is caused by the chemical action of the hot, high pressure and high velocity gases from the propellant in the bore (erosive wear) and by the abrasive action of the driving band as it passes through the barrel. The result is a decrease in the initial resistance to shot start pressure, resulting in a lower maximum pressure and consequently a decrease in muzzle velocity. Wear is reasonably predictable, although it is also normal to measure it regularly, and the consequent difference in muzzle velocity can be calculated and applied to firing data. Thus it need not greatly affect accuracy. However, when barrel wear becomes extreme, unacceptable inconsistencies in muzzle velocity are likely to occur. Additionally, if the rifling is badly worn the projectile driving band is likely to fail, leading to inadequate stability of the projectile, with consequential increased drag and reduced range. This latter effect is random and unpredictable, so it cannot be applied as a correction to firing data.

Erosive wear is often localised at points of imperfection in the bore and at any point where there is a failure in the seal between the driving band and the rifling, when it is termed erosive scoring. This can appear and develop quickly. Annular erosion appears in QF equipment as a localised, circular enlargement of the bore around the forward edge of the cartridge case. Abrasive wear will gradually remove the metal from the surface of the bore, in particular on the driving side of the lands, and it will round the lands. It can be prevented or at least decreased by ammunition design to reduce the friction in the bore. However, erosive wear is normally the most significant form of wear, especially in guns firing at long ranges and at high rates of fire.

There are various methods of reducing wear: an isolating thermal layer can be formed on the surface of the bore by the addition of wear additives; cooler propellants can be used; the barrel can be made from steel with high erosive resistance; or the barrel can be plated with materials such as chromium or molybdenum. Wear additives such as a mixture of magnesium silicate and wax can be applied to the chamber behind the projectile, and they coat the bore as the shell is fired. However, this process should ideally be renewed regularly, which could be impractical. If a cooler burning propellant is used, additional quantities are likely to be required in order to achieve a given maximum pressure and this will mean that the chamber must be larger. Plating is probably the most promising technique, but it is difficult to apply to large calibre barrels and is therefore expensive. Furthermore, if it is not applied well, abrasive wear can begin to strip it.

Wear can also be reduced by water- or air-cooling, although the resulting problems of increased weight, volume and complexity render this technique unsuitable for many applications, especially towed guns. However, the need to consider assisted cooling to prevent overheating in barrels subjected to very high rates of fire may encourage interest in this technique, which is discussed further in Chapter 7.

Barrel Fatigue

Barrel fatigue is the term used to refer to the propagation of cracks beginning in the bore of the barrel and radiating outwards. Their existence is due to the use of steels with high yield strengths, which are needed to contain very high bore pressures but which consequently have low fracture toughness. This low toughness means that the expansion of tiny cracks or crazing found in most gun bores is accelerated when high pressures are applied. Ultimately, catastrophic failure of the barrel could occur well before the wear life is reached. Obviously the safe fatigue life of a barrel needs to be predicted, but it is very difficult to be precise in this area and regular inspections should still be made to spot large cracks. In design, the right balance between fracture toughness and yield strength must be achieved, but decreasing the latter will imply an increase in barrel weight which is normally highly undesirable.

Breech Mechanisms

A breech mechanism closes the end of the barrel after the round has been loaded, carries the firing mechanism, and withstands the rearward firing thrust of the propellant gases. In Breech Loading (BL) guns it carries the means of obturation, while in Quick Firing (QF) guns it supports the cartridge case once loaded and provides the means of extracting the case after firing. The breech must be safe and it should be as simple, reliable, durable and as easy and fast to use as possible. The safety requirements will be such that it must be impossible for the gun to be fired unless the breech is fully closed and also that the breech must not open accidentally during firing. Obviously it is highly desirable that the breech should be readily mass-produced and that servicing and component replacement should be easy. All these demands must be met over a wide range of climatic conditions.

Types of Breech Mechanisms

There are two basic types of breech designs: screw mechanisms and sliding block mechanisms. Screw mechanisms are usually, but not always, fitted to BL systems while sliding blocks are usually used with QF equipment. There are many variations on the basic designs, some of which are discussed in this chapter.

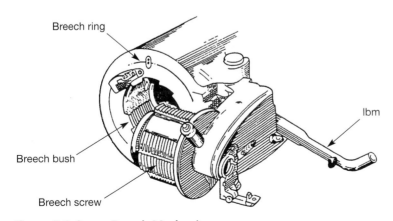

Breech ring

lbm

Breech bush

Breech screw

Figure 5.6 Screw Breech Mechanism

Screw Breeches

A diagram of a typical screw breech is shown in Figure 5.6. The breech screw is held in a carrier attached to the breech ring. The carrier can be mounted to one side or above or below the ring, in order to allow the screw to swing freely during opening and closing. On closing, the breech screw engages in corresponding threads in the inner surface of the breech ring. To allow it to enter and be retracted, the threads are not continuous but have alternate sections cut away and hence they are termed 'interrupted threads'. After the carrier has swung fully home, the screw rotates automatically to engage with the breech ring threads, or the lever breech mechanism (LBM) rotates the screw. Either way, this provides a strong lock against longitudinal pressure when the propellant fires. The pitch of the thread ensures that friction will prevent the breech screw from rotating and opening when the gun is fired.

Figure 5.7 shows the means of obturation provided in a conventional screw mechanism. The charge is contained in a combustible material, normally a fabric bag or light case, but there is no metal cartridge case. The obturator is a truncated cone resilient pad, normally made of neoprene, and is secured to the screw by the mushroom head and the bolt vent axial.

On firing, the mushroom head is forced to the rear by the chamber pressure and in so doing it squeezes the pad which then expands radially against the chamber, thereby forming a tight seal. Since the pad has a hole in it, through

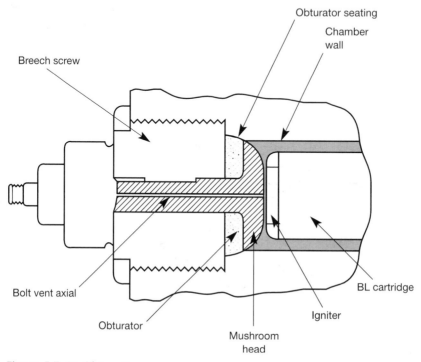

Figure 5.7 BL Obturation

which the bolt vent axial passes, it has a smaller surface area than the mushroom head. Consequently the pressure acting on it is greater than that in the chamber, and this improves the seal. This principle is known as 'intensification'. Thus in BL obturated guns a non-combustible cartridge case is not required, which saves weight and the problem of disposal. A further advantage is that for a given performance the screw mechanism can be lighter than a sliding block because longitudinal firing stresses are distributed over the whole of the firing threads. However, the mechanism is relatively complex and slow to operate compared to most sliding block mechanisms, and it is not easily adaptable for automatic or semi-automatic loading.

Sliding Block Breeches

In a sliding block breech (shown in Figure 5.8) the block moves either vertically or horizontally to close the chamber. If ammunition obturation (provided by a cartridge case) is in use the mechanism can be relatively simple, fast to operate and well suited to automation. A sliding block mechanism is also safer than a screw breech, because there is less chance of the loader's hand being caught in the breech during closing: a hand would tend to be swept away as the block slides home.

As well as requiring a cartridge case to provide rear obturation, a sliding block breech would need to be heavier than a screw breech to withstand equivalent chamber pressure. However, their faster operation makes them attractive for light calibre guns (105mm and below) where the weight and size of the cartridge case does not effectively limit the rate of fire. The choice of a vertical or

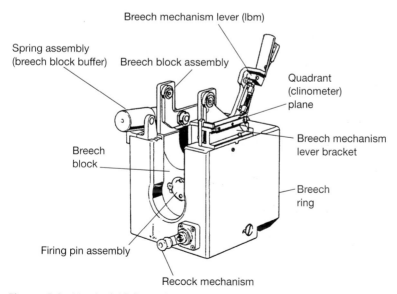

Figure 5.8 Vertical Sliding Block Breech

horizontal sliding block is usually determined by the space available for loading drills around the ordnance. A vertical block normally offers more scope in this respect but a horizontal block requires less effort to operate.

Breech rings for sliding blocks can be of the tied jaw, open jaw or closed jaw type, as shown in Figure 5.9. Tied jaw breech rings are inherently much stronger than open jaw rings because their shape makes it easier to provide the rigidity needed to withstand firing loads. However, they are more expensive to manufacture because it is more difficult to cut a rectangular hole than a slot. Closed jaw breeches are stronger still but they are heavier and restrict access, and are rarely used. All types have one or more pairs of guide slots that mate with ribs on the sliding block as it opens and closes. The ribs and slots are inclined so that a small amount of forward travel is achieved when the breech is closed, thus ensuring that the cartridge case is firmly supported in the chamber.

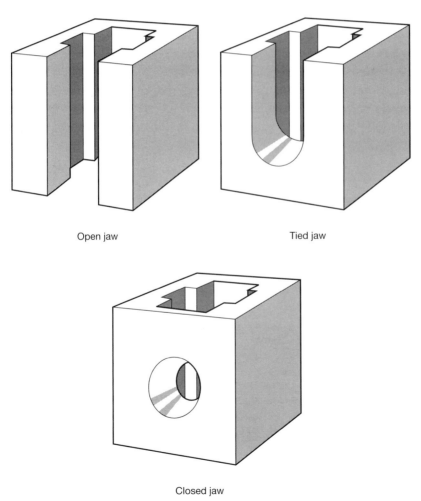

Open jaw   Tied jaw

Closed jaw

Figure 5.9 Open Jaw, Tied Jaw and Closed Jaw Sliding Block Breech Rings

The rear faces of the guide slots are generally designed to accept the rearward firing loads. The loads can be distributed over a greater area of the breech ring if more than one pair of slots is provided, but this requires expensive, high tolerance machining to ensure that all surfaces, accept part of the load. However, regardless of the number of thrust surfaces, this type of breech cannot match the efficiency with which the interrupted threads of a screw mechanism can distribute the firing loads. Hence for a given load the sliding block mechanism will be heavier.

QF, or ammunition obturation, is normally used in conventional sliding block mechanisms. The propellant is contained in a slightly tapered case, and hence the gases it produces on burning are prevented from rearward escape by that case. On firing, the gas pressure expands the case to a tight fit in the chamber, so it must be made of a material resilient enough to expand and then contract to allow easy removal from the chamber. The US Army generally uses steel cases, while in Britain a brass alloy of 70% copper and 30% zinc is used, and in Switzerland plastic cases with a brass base have been employed. A primer is fitted into the base of the case to provide ignition of the propellant. A diagram of the system is shown in Figure 5.10.

As higher chamber pressures are used to provide longer ranges, the use of metal cases with adequate material properties becomes more difficult. If the case is overstrained it can become difficult to extract and the problem is exacerbated if the case is made longer to contain more propellant. Extraction problems will seriously degrade the rate of fire and thus remove one of the prime advantages of sliding block mechanisms: ease and speed of operation.

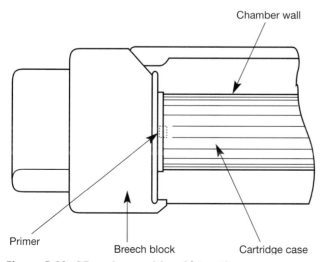

Chamber wall

Primer

Breech block

Cartridge case

Figure 5.10 QF, or Ammunition Obturation

The extractors fitted to a conventional sliding block breech perform two functions. They must unseat the cartridge case after firing and then eject the case. In some equipment they also hold the breech block in the open position. The extractors must satisfy several requirements:

- They must allow for smooth, powerful and relatively slow initial movement to unseat the cartridge case.
- The cartridge case must maintain alignment with the axis of the bore as it is being withdrawn from the chamber.
- The rim of the case must not be damaged as it is being unseated and ejected.
- The final movement of the extractors to eject the case should be fast enough to throw it safely clear of the breech.
- The extractors should not bounce as the breech is opened.

To remove the problem of the cartridge case, breech obturation has now been designed into sliding breeches by the addition of either a metal ring gas seal or an obturator pad similar to that used in a screw breech. The metal seal (as used in the FH70) needs regular cleaning and replacement due to gas erosion and has only shown limited success. The obturator pad and mushroom head are moved vertically and then horizontally to provide the required seal, this being known as a split-block breech. Figure 5.11 shows an example. Such a breech is used in the AS90; it is more complex than other sliding breeches but it provides both a far better seal and greater reliability, especially at high pressures.

Firing Mechanisms

Firing mechanisms can be of the percussion type, or electrical, a combination of both or a modern variation of the electrical type using a laser. In British

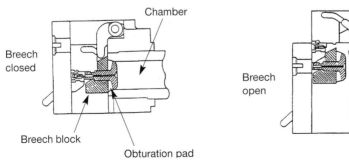

Figure 5.11 A Split-block Breech

service QF equipment has firing mechanisms while those fitted to BL equipment are termed locks. However, in the US there is no such distinction and either term can be used with either type of obturation. British terminology is used in this section.

In a percussion mechanism, a firing pin hits an ignition tube or primer which in turn initiates the charge. In BL equipment the lock is attached to the rear of the bolt vent axial (see Figure 5.7) and holds an ignition tube. The lock contains a striker which hits the tube to ignite it. On initiation the tube fires burning pellets of gun powder through the bolt vent axial to ignite the propellant charge. In QF equipment the firing mechanism is contained in the breech block and has a firing pin which strikes a primer housed in the base of the cartridge case. In either case a firing lever or lanyard is used to release the striker or pin. All mechanisms or locks have some form of safety catch, and they need to be recocked after they have been activated. This can be either automatic or manually operated.

An electrical mechanism sends current to heat a wire in the primer, causing the primer to ignite and thus to initiate the charge. A QF mechanism will contain an insulated needle which carries the current to the primer. Safety is provided by an interruption in the electrical circuit. Combination mechanisms use a percussion device to generate the electrical charge. A laser firing mechanism is most likely to be used with BL equipment, where the laser beam will fire down the tube vent axial to ignite a primer pad on the base of the main propellant charge bag.

In general, the electrical mechanism, compared to the percussion type, is simpler, lighter and more compact, mechanically more reliable, less prone to wear, easier to test and has a much faster response. However, it requires more cleaning and is more susceptible to climatic conditions that could introduce moisture or dirt into the system.

Fume Extractors

In order to allow acceptable working conditions inside the turret of self-propelled guns, a fume extractor is normally provided to prevent propellant fumes being emitted from the breech after it is opened. The extractor is a cylindrical device fitted around the barrel, at about the mid-point, and its hollow interior is connected to the bore by small tubes pointing towards the muzzle, as shown in Figure 5.12. On firing, fumes are forced into the extractor by the high bore pressure after the shell has passed the tubes. Gas flow ceases when the pressure in the extractor is equal to the pressure in the bore.

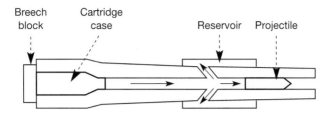

1. Gas drawn into reservoir as projectile passes.

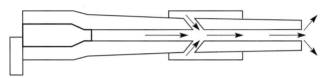

2. Projectile ejected from muzzle and gas drawn from reservoir and expelled from muzzle.

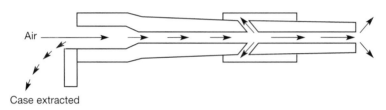

3. Breech opened, cartridge case ejected (if used). Air drawn into bore through breech and expelled from muzzle. Reservoir purged of gas.

Figure 5.12 Operation of a Fume Extractor

As the shell exits from the muzzle the pressure in the barrel drops rapidly and the high pressure fumes exit from the extractor towards the muzzle. This then causes fumes remaining in the chamber to be sucked forward, and the barrel is finally purged by air also moving forward if the breech is opened immediately on run-out. The size of the fume extractor's reservoir and the inclination and dimensions of the nozzles must be designed to allow for the purging cycle to commence before the breech is opened. Rather more complicated extractors have been designed, using a second set of nozzles inclined towards the breech. These contain valves which allow gas in but not out. The aim is to improve the collection efficiency of the gas in cases where pressures and barrel dimensions require it.

Muzzle Brakes

A muzzle brake consists of one or a series of baffles mounted on the end of the barrel which divert some of the propellant gases outwards and rearwards, the resulting change of gas momentum giving a forward force on the barrel in order to reduce recoil. Normally the brake is screwed onto the barrel with a thread opposite to the rifling twist in order to prevent unscrewing when the gun is fired. A locking ring and/or key is usually also provided. On some equipment the brake is made as an integral part of the barrel.

There are many different designs and methods of construction of muzzle brakes. Several slots or baffles can be included and, together with their angle to the axis of the bore and their area, this provides the means of achieving the desired efficiency of the brake. Some examples are shown in Figure 5.13. Built-up muzzle brakes consist of several plates which are bolted or welded together. Swaged brakes are made from a single forging which is swaged or drawn to shape and then machined. Muzzle brakes can also be cast, but in most modern high performance equipment the brake is now machined from a single forging. Although such brakes are relatively expensive, modern computer-controlled machine tools make construction fairly easy and such a muzzle brake is probably the most durable type.

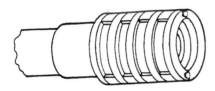

Built-up construction

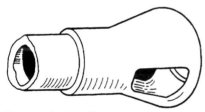

Swaged single baffle.

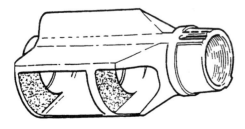

Machined solid forging

Figure 5.13 Muzzle Brakes

Operation and Advantages

When the gun is fired, the propellant gases moving behind the projectile expand and strike the baffles of the muzzle brake, thus exerting a force acting in a forward direction, as shown in Figure 5.14. This force acts against the recoil force of the gun, thus reducing the trunnion pull and so improving stability (as discussed later in this chapter). There are various alternative advantages. The recoil distance could be reduced, or a higher charge could be fired than would otherwise be possible, or a smaller recoil mechanism could be used, or a larger ordnance could use the same carriage or mounting.

Efficiency

Theoretically, the maximum force exerted by the gases would be achieved if they could all be deflected through 180°. However, some of the gas will always follow the projectile out of the muzzle, and friction and turbulence will further reduce the effect. In addition, if the gases were deflected through 180° they could seriously endanger the gun detachment, and in order to allow the gases to expand to maximum velocity the brake would need to be about 25 times the calibre of the barrel. Consequently there are many constraints on efficiency.

Muzzle brakes are usually designed for efficiencies of between 20% and 80%. In order to achieve high efficiency several baffles are used, although since each baffle can only deflect at most 60% of the gas that reaches it, the number of baffles is rarely more than two or three unless they have a small surface area. It should be noted that part of the reduction in recoil energy is simply due to the mass of the muzzle brake, which of course adds to the recoiling mass.

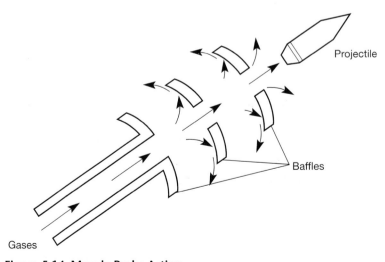

Figure 5.14 Muzzle Brake Action

Disadvantages

A high efficiency brake is heavy and can cause ordnance balancing problems, especially if retro-fitted, when corrections for muzzle velocity, jump and droop will also need to be made. Gases deflected by any brake can cause obscuration around the gun, which is why the baffles are only normally at the sides, although this still degrades concealment and will be a particular problem in the direct fire role. However, the most serious problem is that the blast from the muzzle brake will cause high overpressures around the gun, notably to the rear and close to both sides. This is particularly undesirable for towed guns where the detachments have no physical protection compared to a self-propelled gun where they are inside the turret or behind the chassis. Fortunately, towed guns have more space available to accommodate a long recoil stroke – typically up to 2m – and hence less need to reduce recoil length than self-propelled equipment, where volume tends to be a limitation. Consequently towed guns can more easily accept lower efficiency brakes. Nevertheless, blast effects will still be large enough to warrant the need for effective ear protection such as muffs or plugs to avoid ear drum damage. They can also affect the thorax and vital organs, and cause fatigue in detachment members.

SECTION 2 – CARRIAGES AND MOUNTINGS

A carriage or mounting is a combination of assemblies that supports the ordnance, points it in the correct direction for firing and provides stability for the whole gun. In the case of a mobile equipment, it may also provide the means of transportation.

A carriage fires with its wheels in contact with the ground, while a mounting does not. A mobile mounting travels on its wheels but raises or removes them before firing, using a plate or girders to support the weapon in action. A self-propelled mounting is fixed to a wheeled or tracked chassis with its own motive power. Examples of each type of support are shown in Figures 5.15 to 5.18.

There are two other categories of mountings which are mentioned here for historical completeness only since they are currently obsolete. Static mountings were used for equipment which had no wheels, were permanently mounted and were effectively immobile. Semi-mobile mountings could be moved but required specially prepared sites. These types of artillery were used for some elements of coastal, garrison, railway and early air defence systems as part of fixed defences.

The main two parts of a carriage or mounting are its 'basic structure' and its 'superstructure'. Generally, the whole superstructure moves when the ordnance is traversed, while the basic structure remains static once in action.

Figure 5.15 The British Light Gun – an example of a Carriage

Figure 5.16 The Russian D30 – an example of a Mounting

Figure 5.17 The American M109 – an example of a Tracked SP Mounting

Figure 5.18 The South African G6 – an example of a Wheeled SP Mounting

THE SUPERSTRUCTURE

The main parts of the superstructure are the saddle, the traversing and elevating gears, the balancing gears, the cradle, the recoil system and the sights. These are shown in the diagram at Figure 5.19.

General Configuration

The function of the superstructure is to support the ordnance and provide the means of pointing it in the required direction. The cradle supports the barrel and houses the recoil mechanism to which the barrel is connected. Trunnions are fixed to both sides of the cradle and fit into horizontal bearings in the saddle, so that the cradle and ordnance (which form the elevating mass) can rotate in a vertical plane. The saddle rests on the saddle support which is part of the basic structure and it generally has a vertical pivot to allow the entire superstructure to rotate in a horizontal plane. The trunnions are not normally at the centre of gravity of the elevating mass so the latter is normally out of balance. To overcome this and allow easy elevation and depression, the balancing gear is connected between the cradle and the saddle.

The Cradle

The cradle has grooves to support the ordnance and allow it to move backwards during recoil and forwards during run-out (the movement of the recoiling parts back to their pre-firing position). There are basically three types. A trough cradle is a U-shaped box below the ordnance which also contains the recoil mechanism. It thus provides some protection from shell splinters and small arms fire to the lower half of the barrel and to the whole recoil mechanism. The grooves or guideways run along the full length of the upper surfaces of the trough. The front end of the trough is blocked off by the cradle cap to which the recoil mechanism piston rods are attached.

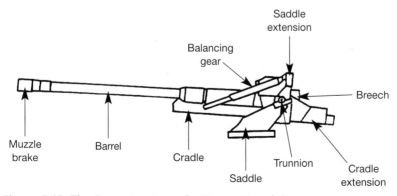

Figure 5.19 The Superstructure of a Conventional Gun

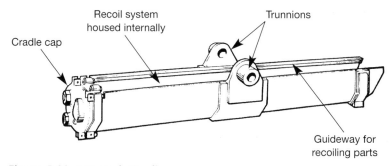

Cradle cap

Recoil system
housed internally

Trunnions

Guideway for
recoiling parts

Figure 5.20 A Trough Cradle

The second type is a ring cradle which is a cylinder around part of the barrel and these two components are in contact throughout recoil and run-out. Usually the inner surface of the cradle is fitted with sleeves or pads against which the barrel slides and which can normally be lubricated or replaced. The ring cradle has external housings for the recoil system and the piston rods are connected to a flange on the barrel. A ring cradle is generally shorter, more compact, lighter and easier to manufacture than a trough. However, it provides less protection for the recoil mechanism. Furthermore, the clearance between the barrel and the cradle is critical: too small and the barrel might jam; too large and the barrel is likely to vibrate, with potential wear and accuracy problems.

The third type is an open structure cradle, which is basically a cross between the trough and ring types. It is used where keeping the weight light is a high priority and a good example is seen on the British Light Gun in Figure 5.15.

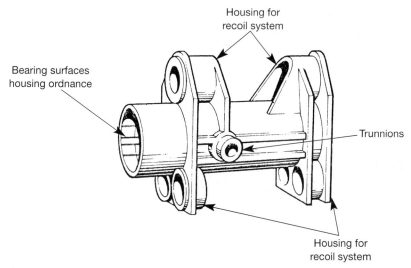

Housing for
recoil system

Bearing surfaces
housing ordnance

Trunnions

Housing for
recoil system

Figure 5.21 A Ring Cradle

The Saddle

As mentioned earlier, the saddle supports the cradle by means of trunnion bearings, which allow the cradle and ordnance to be elevated in a vertical plane. Capsquares form the top of the bearings, providing firm retention of the cradle while also allowing it to be removed if necessary. When in action, the saddle must obviously be free to rotate to allow easy traverse so the vertical pivot on its base must be strong enough to withstand the shear stress resulting from firing. However, there must be an arrangement for holding down the saddle so that it does not tilt due to either the recoil forces when firing or vibration when travelling.

Some guns were designed without a saddle, having instead cross axle traverse. Here the trail supported the cradle directly and the ordnance was traversed by moving it across the wheel axles. This arrangement allowed only limited traverse and is not used in modern designs.

Stability and Strength

Before discussing the next component of the superstructure, the recoil mechanism, it is necessary to consider the problem of gun stability. Gun designers try to ensure that when a gun fires the recoil energy is absorbed in a way that

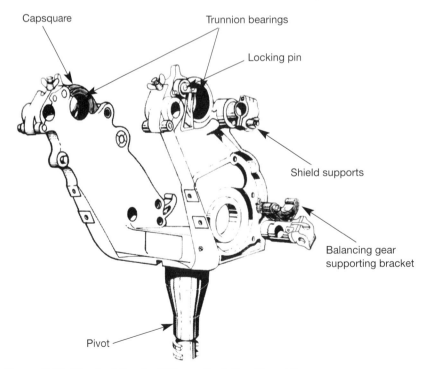

Figure 5.22 The Saddle of a 105mm Pack Howitzer L5

allows the carriage or mounting to remain stable. A gun can be regarded as stable if the main supports of the carriage or mounting remain stationary during both recoil and run-out. A high level of stability is required for several reasons: excessive movement will affect accuracy and consistency, and it will require the gun to be repositioned or at least relaid, hence reducing the rate of fire. Poor stability is likely to affect the confidence of the detachment and ultimately it could damage the gun.

The Components of Stability

Stability can easily be increased by making the gun heavier (e.g. compare the AS90 at 45 tons with the M109A2 at 25 tons) but for high mobility, lightweight equipment other techniques must be used. To see how, the components of stability must be considered. When a gun fires, two forces and moments are acting in opposition and their relative size will determine the degree of stability. These are shown in Figure 5.23, which gives a simplified illustration of the weight (W) and recoil force (R) acting on the gun. By taking moments about the point at which the end of the trail is in contact with the ground, it can be seen that if WxL is greater than RxH then the wheels or platform of the gun will remain in contact with the ground and the gun should have adequate stability.

In modern guns the recoil energy is so large that without a recoil mechanism to dissipate it the weight of the gun would be inadequate to counter its effects. The recoil mechanism reduces the instantaneous force by applying it over a finite time. Stability is concerned with the force applied at the trunnions, which is therefore known as the 'trunnion pull'. A further consideration is the direction in which the trunnion pull acts, which is in line with the axis of the bore.

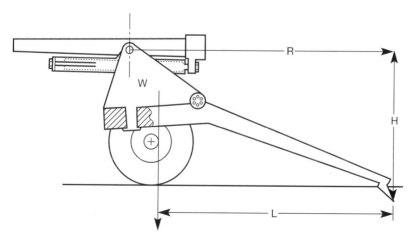

Figure 5.23 Simplified Stability Assessment for a Gun

The Gun remains stable if WxL > RxH

Consequently, as the barrel is elevated the overturning moment is reduced. Once the bore axis is pointing within the contact area or 'foundation figure' of the gun with the ground, stability should not be a problem. It should also be noted that instability tends to increase at large deflections from the centre of traverse since the bore axis could point outside the foundation figure, and this may limit the area that the gun can engage without platform adjustment.

Nevertheless, a gun must be designed for the worst case of stability, i.e. direct firing with a near-horizontal, or even depressed, barrel. The equation in Figure 5.23 means that for maximum stability the trail length should be long and the trunnion height should be low. There are other methods of avoiding instability. Spades are normally used at the ends of the trails to increase resistance to movement, and they can be used on an SP mounting, although they do take time to deploy. Recoil energy can also be reduced by using a muzzle brake as discussed earlier in this chapter. If necessary, limitations can be placed on the degree of traverse and the minimum elevation at which higher charges are fired.

Yet another method is to lengthen the recoil distance, giving more time over which the energy can be dissipated. However, a long recoil will reduce the rate of fire of the gun and for an SP gun it could increase the dimensions of the turret and chassis, so it should be as short as necessary to ensure stability and strength. In this respect the fact that stability increases with elevation can be used to advantage. Guns are often designed with a simple mechanism to reduce recoil length as elevation is increased. For an SP mounting this allows the height of the chassis or turret to be minimised. For a towed gun it could obviate the need for digging a recoil pit which might otherwise be needed to ensure that the breech did not hit the ground during recoil.

Another factor to be considered in gun stability is 'jump'. This is defined as the displacement between the axis of the bore before and after firing. On firing, the force produced by the charge is exerted along the bore axis. Unless the centre of gravity of the recoiling parts remains on this axis a force couple will be set up which will move these parts in the plane containing the axis and the centre of gravity. Jump can be predicted and firing data can be adjusted to minimise its effects on accuracy.

Strength

Before discussing recoil systems, another factor which drives their need is that of the strength of the structure, particularly around the trunnions and also either through the trails or around the turret ring. If there was an inadequate recoil system then the firing forces would all be transmitted through the trunnions and the turret ring or trails, which would require them to be very strong and therefore heavy or made of expensive materials.

Recoil Systems

All guns have recoil mechanisms which cause most of the recoil energy to dissipate as heat on firing. They perform a wide range of tasks connected with this function. They hold the ordnance in the run-out position whatever the elevation of the barrel; they return the ordnance to its firing position; and they control the run-out to avoid large impact forces as it returns.

The recoil cycle is as follows. After firing, once the chamber pressure has increased to the point where the projectile begins to move forwards, the ordnance begins to move rearwards in reaction. This recoil continues until after the projectile has left the barrel and the gas pressure has reduced to atmospheric. Run-out then begins, as the energy stored in the recoil system is released. Run-out is controlled, increasingly so in the final stages so that there is no jarring as the ordnance returns to its firing position, which could cause damage and disturb the lay of the gun for bearing and elevation or even cause the gun to tip forwards. The recoil cycle is complete when the ordnance has stopped in its original position. The main components of the mechanism are the buffer – which dissipates some recoil energy – and the recuperator – which stores some – added to which will be a device for controlling run-out, cut-off gears to vary the length of recoil, and an oil reservoir to replenish the buffer.

The Buffer

The buffer controls the rearward movement of the recoiling parts and in modern equipment is invariably hydraulic. Figure 5.24 shows a simple example of how it works.

A piston inside the buffer is connected directly to the barrel. As the ordnance recoils, oil in the buffer is forced through apertures in the piston and some of the recoil energy is converted to heat in the oil. The size of the apertures is such that oil cannot pass through quickly enough to relieve the pressure behind the piston head, and hence the buffer is able to retard the piston and thereby check the recoil.

It is desirable to decrease the recoil velocity uniformly. If the size of the aperture can be varied so that it narrows when the velocity increases and widens as the velocity decreases, the hydraulic pressure in the buffer cylinder can be kept constant throughout. This will create a constant resistance and maintain constant deceleration. Automatically varying the size of the apertures can be achieved by altering the shape of the cylinder walls and/or the shape of the piston head, or by the use of tapered rods or slots along the walls.

As discussed earlier in this chapter, it may be necessary to vary the recoil length with the angle of elevation, since a long recoil is normally not desirable (for reasons of gun height) or needed (for stability) at high angles of elevation.

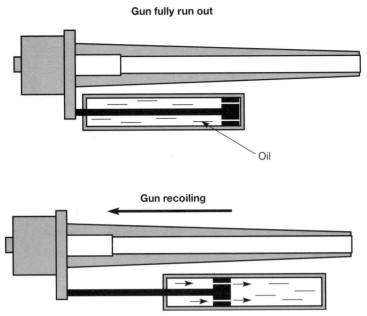

Figure 5.24 Hydraulic Buffer Action

This can be achieved by a relatively simple mechanical arrangement called a cut-off gear, which uses levers connected between the buffer and the saddle to adjust automatically the apertures in the buffer as the ordnance is elevated.

The Recuperator

The recuperator is the mechanism that stores sufficient energy to return the recoiled parts to their original firing position and holds them there until the next round is fired. A simple example of a recuperator is shown in Figure 5.25. This shows that the recuperator is a cylinder containing a spring and a piston connected to the barrel. During recoil the spring is compressed by the piston, thus storing some of the recoil energy. At the end of recoil the spring expands and pushes the piston forward which in turn moves the barrel back to the run-out position. The spring can be a metallic coil or compressed gas, or a combination of both. The buffer and recuperator are normally separated but it is possible to combine their functions into one cylinder.

Control of Final Run-Out

As mentioned earlier, the final stages of run-out should be smooth and controlled in order to prevent damage as the ordnance comes to rest. This is normally achieved by incorporating a control device at the end of the main buffer or in a completely separate buffer. Figure 5.26 shows how this works. As the piston moves to the end of run-out it passes into a hollow rod, thus

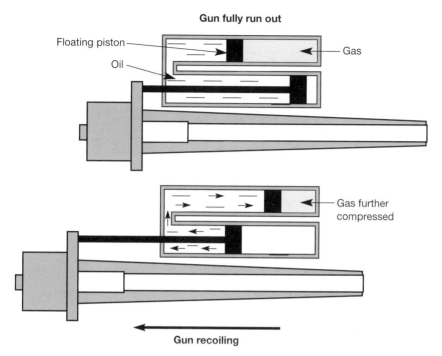

Figure 5.25 A Recuperator

effectively creating an additional annular aperture through which some of the remaining oil must flow. This causes extra resistance, which thereby increases deceleration until the piston is brought to rest.

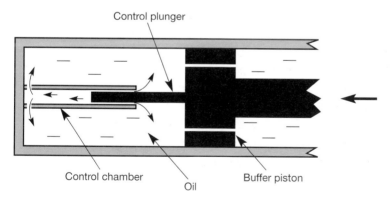

Figure 5.26 A Control to Run Out

Oil Reservoirs
In order to keep the buffer filled with oil, some form of reservoir is required. This can simply be a tank mounted above the level of the buffer which feeds it

87

by gravity. Alternatively it can be a 'replenisher' which is a cylinder filled with oil and kept under pressure by a spring-loaded or gas-filled piston, which force-feeds the buffer.

Soft Recoil

If the ordnance is already moving forward when the gun fires, some of the recoil force will be used up in overcoming the forward momentum of the moving parts. The recoil energy to be absorbed will therefore be reduced. This should lead to a variety of advantages in lower weight and smaller dimensions for the complete equipment. The concept involves holding the ordnance under tension on a latch at maximum recoil; the latch is released and the gun fires automatically as the breech passes a specific point. The principle is used in many small arms, such as the SMG, and is known as soft recoil when applied to artillery.

There are, however, a number of critical design problems that need to be overcome. The first is the possibility of misfires, where some form of buffer would be required to prevent the ordnance travelling too far forwards and tipping the gun over. A means of returning the gun to its latch position would also be required. Secondly, unlike in small arms, allowance has to be made for firing a variety of charges. At higher charges the recoiling parts have to move further forward to allow the greater recoil to be absorbed. If they moved the same distance before firing at lower charges there would be insufficient recoil to reach the latch position. Thus an arrangement must be provided for firing the gun at various barrel positions during the run forward. Since this is likely to be set manually, allowance for incorrect drills must be made, such as fitting a buffer in case recoil is excessive due to a wrong setting. Finally, the natural variation in ignition delay on firing must be accepted by providing a safety margin on ordnance travel.

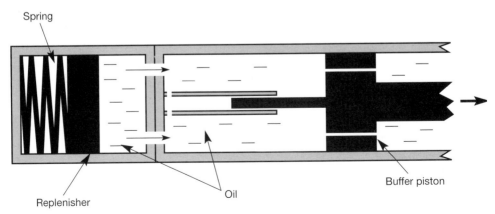

Fig 5.27 A Replenisher

Figure 5.28 The US M204 105mm Howitzer

Soft recoil was developed for the M204 105mm Howitzer in the USA as part of a programme to field a lightweight howitzer. This was not introduced into service, partly because the competitive British Light Gun could fire to greater range (17km compared to 11.5km) and was an equivalent weight. It seems unlikely to be used now because the 105mm calibre is not considered adequate and 155mm guns can be produced to an acceptable weight.

Balancing Gears

As mentioned earlier, the trunnions are not usually sited at the centre of gravity of the ordnance but are normally behind it, closer to the breech. This allows more of the ordnance to be mounted forward of the area used by the detachment serving the gun, thus giving them more room to move. This is particularly useful on SP equipment. Furthermore, at high angles of elevation the breech will be higher off the ground, thus making loading easier and reducing the need for short recoil. Finally, rear trunnions may permit a lower silhouette and so aid concealment.

Since the ordnance is therefore out of balance, some form of balancing gears are required. These operate by tension or compression, the type being determined by the nature of the force acting on the arm connected to the ordnance. The spring which provides the counter to the out of balance moment of the ordnance is, however, normally always in compression. An example of each type is shown in Figure 5.29.

Metal springs are simple and reliable but a spring and gas combination (a pneumatic spring) is often used. The pneumatic spring is generally smaller but is more susceptible to failure if damaged and may have to be adjusted for different climatic conditions.

Elevating and Traversing Gears

Elevating Gears
The elevating mass consists of the ordnance, the recoil mechanism and the cradle. It is linked to the saddle by the elevating gear, the purpose of which is

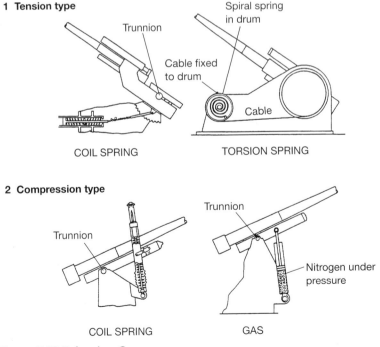

Figure 5.29 Balancing Gears

to transmit and control the movement of the elevating mass relative to the saddle. Elevating gears must obviously be conveniently located, simple and easy to operate. They must also be non-reversible so that the ordnance cannot elevate or depress on its own, and they must allow fine control for accurate adjustment (or 'laying') while being strong enough to transmit some of the firing stresses. In order to minimise stress on the gear, it should either be in the same vertical plane as the axis of the bore – normally directly under the barrel – or two gears should be provided, one on either side of the ordnance. Cradle or barrel clamps are often provided to hold the ordnance rigid while the gun is in transit and thus avoid wear due to vibration on the elevating gear.

Gears can be manual or power driven (either electric or hydraulic), but the latter are mainly limited to SP equipment because the power requirements are such that a generator or hydraulic pump must be running continuously. A simple gear train is usually employed, but this can be interrupted on some equipment by a 'quick loading gear'. This allows the ordnance to be brought to a specific elevation, known as the loading angle, independent of the sights to make loading easier while laying drills continue simultaneously. Such an arrangement assists in maintaining high rates of fire at all elevation angles. An alternative is to have two elevating gears: a coarse set for rapid elevation, and a fine set for accurate final laying. When they can be employed, power drives are usually best but it should be easy to engage a reversionary manual drive in case of power failure.

Traversing Gears

A traversing gear is a mechanism for moving the superstructure in the horizontal plane, by shifting the saddle relative to the basic structure. Like elevating gears, traversing gears must allow fine control, be non-reversible (in case the saddle is not horizontal and tries to turn due to gravitational forces) and be able to transmit some firing stresses. In this respect the bearings used for the saddle pivot or the gun turret must be able to transmit the firing loads while allowing rapid traverse. Ball or roller bearings are usually employed. Like elevating gears, traversing gears can be manual or power driven, with the option for reversionary manual operation.

Traverse may be limited in order to avoid both instability problems and also the possibility of fouling the basic structure during recoil. The limits will tend to be set by the role: for example if the gun is to have an effective anti-tank capability then wide limits are necessary because the short range can generate large switches in bearing. A towed gun sometimes has a quick release mechanism to allow a large approximate change in bearing to be made rapidly, before the gears are re-engaged for accurate setting of the bearing. Turreted SP guns usually have 6,400 mils traverse but this normally means that access to both the crew compartment and ammunition replenishment is likely to be limited at certain traverse angles. Furthermore, stability limitations may dictate that top charges cannot be fired when the turret is nearly at right angles to the chassis.

Traverse limits are an important factor in gun design, so they need to be considered carefully. The requirement for a large limit is likely to lead to an increase in the size and weight of the gun. It may be better to accept that the basic structure should be moved to accommodate large switches in bearing.

Sights

Indirect Fire
The term 'indirect fire' is used to describe fire applied when the gun is pointed at the target without reference to any visual link that may exist between the sight and the target. Normally there is no such intervisibility at all, this being one means of increasing the survivability of the gun. When a gun is in the indirect fire role the barrel is pointed, or 'layed', in the correct direction by reference to a known bearing for direction (or line), and to the horizontal plane for elevation. The sight used for this is termed a 'dial sight'.

Indirect Fire Optical Sights
For optical sights the known bearing will be to one of three points. The first could be a visible 'gun aiming point' (GAP) such as an easily identifiable object several kilometres away. Secondly, a pair of 'aiming posts' could be used; these are poles which are in line with the sight on the known bearing, and with the first pole equally spaced between the sight and the second pole. Thirdly, a reflection of the sight in a special mirror called a paralleloscope can be used; in this case the sight image is at infinity so this is normally the most accurate method. Reference points are usually chosen to be in preferred general directions from the sight in order to avoid any obscuration by other components of the gun.

When a gun is initially deployed it is positioned with its barrel pointing in a known direction, normally towards the centre of the expected target area. The sight is supported in a bracket which is mounted either on the cradle or on the saddle and linked to the cradle. Although the bearing to the reference point is known, and can be set and read on the sight, it is not actually used when laying. A separate 'slipping scale' is set once the gun has been orientated, and this is then always used to point the barrel on the correct bearing.

The process of laying for line is as follows. When a target bearing is ordered, this is set on the slipping scale by turning the sight. The sight is therefore no longer viewing the reference point. The ordnance is then traversed until the sight optical axis is once again viewing the reference point, and the barrel will now be pointing along the bearing set. This sequence is shown in Figure 5.30.

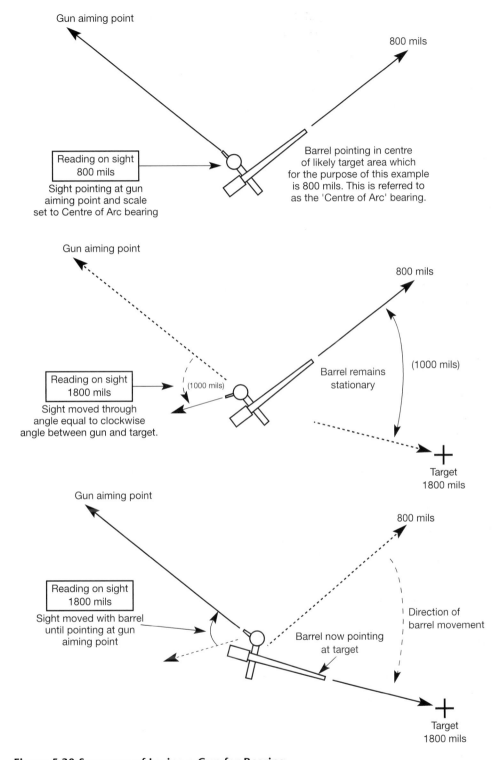

Figure 5.30 Sequence of Laying a Gun for Bearing

The horizontal plane will be indicated by bubbles in tubes or by a set of pointers. To lay for elevation, the ordered elevation or range is set on an appropriate scale. This will mean that the sight optical axis is no longer horizontal. The ordnance is then elevated until the sight is level as indicated by the bubble or pointers. In addition, the sight must always be cross levelled to remove the effect of trunnion tilt if the gun has not been positioned on level ground. To ensure accuracy and consistency a standard sequence of lay should always be used. Typically this is: lay roughly for line, lay roughly for elevation, cross level, then lay accurately for line and then elevation. To avoid errors due to slackness in the gears, the final laying movements should always be in the same direction.

In practice, the barrel is not aimed in the precise direction of the target. It is offset to allow for meteorological ('met') corrections and for 'drift'. Met corrections are incorporated into the ballistic calculation to determine the firing data. Drift is the lateral deviation of the projectile resulting from its spin, the Magnus effect and rotation of the earth. Similarly, the calculation of the angle of elevation must take into account a wide variety of factors including the range, the difference in height between the gun and the target (leading to 'angle of sight'), met, ammunition weight, charge temperature and muzzle velocity. Most of these factors are described in detail in Volume 1 of this series[1]. Some sights were designed to compensate for drift, angle of sight and muzzle velocity, but it is now usual to include compensation for them all in the ballistic calculation of firing data, thus allowing sights to be kept simple.

Electronic Sights

Very modern sights, such as those fitted on the AS90, can be electronic and use a gyroscope to provide both bearing and horizontal reference. They generate two signals when the required bearing and elevation are input to the sight; these are compared with signals generated by the positions of the saddle (or turret) and barrel, and the latter are moved until the signal difference is zero. The indication is usually by a series of lights which are extinguished at zero difference, or by a digital readout of the bearing and elevation, or both. The barrel must then be pointing on the correct bearing and at the correct elevation. Such sighting systems can provide better accuracy than optical systems, since inputting numerical data is less likely to lead to errors than would poor selection of the optical aiming mark by the layer, especially when he is under pressure. When allied to an automatic, powered gun laying system, the combination is also likely to be much faster than manual laying with optical sights.

Direct Fire Sights

Direct fire is always a secondary role for artillery guns. They are preferably deployed out of the direct view of enemy weapons. Consequently if direct fire has to be used the ranges involved are likely to be fairly short, perhaps no more than a few hundred metres. The indirect fire sight can be used but often a direct fire telescope is provided as well. The latter will be essential if electronic sights are used for indirect fire. Arrangements have to be made for the engagement of moving targets and for zeroing for the type of ammunition to be used. This is likely to make the use of the dial sight rather complex and slow compared to the telescope. A telescope will have a graticule pattern inscribed with horizontal lines showing ranges and vertical lines showing leads (the amount of aim-off to allow for the estimated crossing velocity of the target). This will minimise or even eliminate calculations before firing. To achieve maximum target effect the top charge is almost always used: this will give the flattest trajectory and the shortest time of flight, which both improve accuracy, and the greatest kinetic energy when the round hits. Indeed, modern guns have such high muzzle velocities and their standard HE shells have such lethal content that special anti-armour rounds may not be provided. The use of just one charge naturally simplifies the design of the direct fire telescope.

THE BASIC STRUCTURE

As mentioned at the beginning of this chapter, a gun consists of a carriage or mounting and the ordnance. The carriage or mounting in turn are divided into the superstructure and the basic structure. The basic structure supports the superstructure, and horizontal movement between them is controlled by the traversing gear. While the general arrangement of the superstructures of a carriage and a mounting can be similar, the layout of the basic structures of both categories will differ in significant respects.

Carriages

The basic structure of the carriage will include: a saddle support on which the saddle rests; the trails and method of articulation; platforms and spades; and the wheels, axles, suspension and brakes.

Trails

Trails help to hold the gun in the firing position and transmit the recoil forces to the ground. They usually also serve to connect the gun to its towing vehicle (although in some designs a connection at the end of the barrel is provided instead). The rear of the trail is normally fitted with a spade which may be adjustable or removable. There are three types of trail: the pole trail, box trail and split trail.

The pole, or single, trail is the simplest and normally lightest design but is now obsolete. Traverse of the saddle is very limited (to about 150 mils) since the gun would become unstable. Elevation is also very limited (to about 300 mils) due to the likelihood of the breech fouling the trail during recoil.

A box trail is well illustrated by the Light Gun (Figure 5.15). It consists of two members, either parallel (or nearly so) and joined at the rear by a cross member, or splayed, in which case they are joined directly together at the rear as in the Light Gun. Box trails normally allow a top traverse of up to 200 mils either side of centre, depending on how much the side members are splayed. The splayed trails provide little or no impediment to elevation and recoil. They often have a firing platform which is positioned below the gun during deployment and on which the wheels rest. This distributes the weight and firing loads and also facilitates traverse of the whole gun through 6,400 mils, which can normally be accomplished by one man.

A split trail consists of two separate members which are spread as widely as possible to provide stability for a large top traverse. The amount to which they are spread is limited only by the wheels or by trail stops. Top traverse is greater than for a box trail and may be around 600 mils. However, movement of the gun outside traverse limits requires at least two men. Furthermore the effective trail length is shorter than the actual length of the legs due to their split, and when the gun is fired at maximum top traverse most of the firing stresses are taken up by one leg. Consequently the trails are normally longer and heavier than those of a box trail. A gun with split trails could be dismantled more easily for movement in several parts, for example the Italian 105mm Pack Howitzer shown in Figure 5.31.

Figure 5.31 Italian 105mm Pack Howitzer – an Example of Split Trails

The trails may also be connected in a straight line to lower the trunnion height for direct fire.

Articulation

Guns with box trails only have three points of contact with the ground and so can readily remain in contact with rough ground. However, split trail guns have four points of contact and so require articulation or equalisation, a means of providing adequate freedom of movement between the trail legs and the axle or saddle support. This involves pins, rocking arms or ball and socket joints, and hence complicates design. The articulation must be lockable for travelling. There must also be some means of preventing the trails from closing when the gun is in the firing position. Two examples of articulation are shown in Figure 5.32.

1. Longitudinal pivot

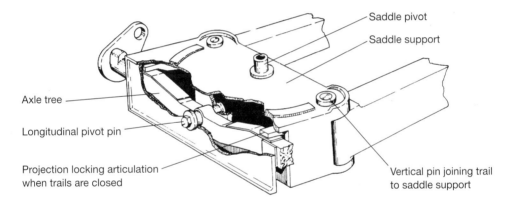

2. Rocking arm.

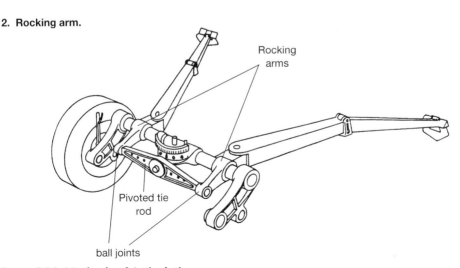

Figure 5.32 Methods of Articulation

Spades

Spades are normally fitted to the end of a trail leg to restrict movement of the gun during recoil. They can be forged, cast or of built-up construction, and can be fixed, detachable or hinged to the trail. The latter two types allow greater movement of the gun when travelling, and hence improve mobility. All types must be designed so that while they transmit horizontal firing stresses efficiently into the ground, they can also be readily removed from the ground to facilitate trail movement when a large amount of traverse is needed. A small spade will be light and so is easier to remove from the ground than a large spade, but it will tend to move soil more and so be less efficient. The spade design and size is determined largely by the types of soil in which it is likely to operate. In practice, most guns are likely to be deployed on a wide variety of soils with very different bearing strengths, so the design is likely to be a compromise. Some guns are provided with two designs and sizes of spades to allow for the variation in soil type.

Platforms

Platforms are usually fitted to equipment on which the trails cannot absorb the firing stresses enough to prevent excessive movement. They are connected to the gun by wire stays or rigid brackets and are deployed under the wheels, so they must obviously be raised for travelling. They assist in transmitting the vertical components of recoil energy to the ground by providing a larger contact area and hence reducing ground pressure. Secondly, due to friction and by digging into the ground slightly they help to prevent the gun running backwards, and finally they provide a base on which the wheels can easily run when the trails are being moved.

Axles

Axles can be underslung or overslung, depending on whether the wheel hub centres are above the axis of the axle or below it. Underslung axles permit a lower weapon silhouette and normally greater stability, but can limit elevation and are more likely to foul the ground when travelling. A long axle permits greater top traverse and greater stability when being towed, but is more cumbersome when travelling. On some designs, such as the 105mm Pack Howitzer, the wheel track can be varied and the axle can be adjusted between overslung for travelling and normal firing and underslung for anti-tank firing. Such versatility is only practicable on lightweight equipment and will be more complex and costly.

Brakes

The brakes on most carriages are of the conventional drum type. They will be activated from the towing vehicle through an electrical or mechanical connection, and will be operated by air, electricity or hydraulics. A hand brake or manual activation of the travelling brakes will also be provided. This assists in preventing movement of the gun when firing and when parked or deployed on slopes. Independent hand brakes on each wheel can assist in manhandling the gun in difficult ground conditions.

Suspensions

Most carriages do not have a full suspension system, the only effect being due to the pneumatic tyres. A gun with suspension, such as the British 105mm Light Gun, is more complex but allows fast towing speeds on roads and cross-country, thus improving tactical mobility.

Mobile Mountings

As mentioned earlier, a mobile mounting is an equipment that travels on wheels but does not fire off them. When the equipment is deployed, the wheels are either removed or raised off the ground. The main advantage of a mobile mounting compared to a carriage is that stability is improved through the use of a solid mounting and the fact that the gun's centre of gravity will be lower when the wheels have been raised or removed. Thus stability is likely to be better than for a carriage, leading to greater accuracy and consistency. A further advantage is that in some cases the whole superstructure can be moved quickly through 6,400 mils without the necessity of moving the basic structure which is in contact with the ground. However, mobile mountings are usually both heavier and slower to deploy and bring out of action than carriages, so they may be less suitable for forces requiring maximum mobility. They also tend to require flat, level ground for deployment.

There are three types of mobile mounting: pedestal and stabilising girders; platform and stabilising girders; and platform and sole plate.

An example of a pedestal and stabilising girders type of construction was shown in Figure 5.16, the Russian D30. The wheels have been raised clear of the ground. Stability is maintained throughout 6,400 mils traverse by the use of three girders at equal horizontal angles, but there is no articulation between the girders and the pedestal, so the gun platform must be on a firm, level site.

In the platform and stabilising girders type of construction, such as is shown in Figure 5.33, the girders act rather like split trails on a carriage, except that they are in contact with the ground throughout their length. Once again, the wheels have been raised and there is no articulation. Spades are normally used to assist in preventing movement when firing.

The platform and sole plate type of mobile mounting (sometimes called a turntable mounting) is used with heavier equipment where mobility is not a high priority. An example is shown in Figure 5.34. A large traversing ring is mounted on the supporting base and the equipment, which is nearly balanced on the ring, can relatively easily be moved through 6,400 mils by raising the

Figure 5.33 Platform and Stabilising Girders on a Mobile Mounting (US 8 Inch Howitzer)

rear with a roller and jack system. The sole plate at the rear of the basic structure permits a limited amount of top traverse.

Self-propelled Mountings

The vehicle chassis provides the basic structure for a Self-propelled (SP) mounting. The saddle is mounted in a traversing race, and the equipment can

Figure 5.34 Platform and Sole Plate Mobile Mounting (German K38)

have limited top traverse, such as the 8 inch M110 shown in Figure 5.35, or 6,400 mils traverse as provided by most turreted guns such as the AS90 shown in Figure 5.36. Guns with a calibre greater than 155mm are unlikely to be mounted in a turret for several reasons: firstly, the large recoil forces will give rise to stresses which are difficult to transmit through the saddle and turret ring without damage; secondly, those forces will make stability difficult to maintain throughout 6,400 mils of traverse; and, thirdly, handling of heavy ammunition – around 90kg for an 8 inch gun – would be extremely difficult inside a turret.

On firing, horizontal movement is restricted or eliminated by the weight of the equipment and the length of track or area of wheels in contact with the ground. Rear spades are sometimes provided to improve stability (as seen in Figure 5.35). These are generally needed on large calibre guns (in excess of 155mm) due to the large recoil forces resulting from firing heavy shells to long ranges, and on lighter weight guns. For example, the US M109 weighs around 26 tons and needs spades while the British AS90 (also 155mm) weighs 48 tons and does not. Wheeled SP guns may be provided with stabilisers for similar reasons. It is interesting to note that the South African G6 (Figure 5.18) weighs the same as the AS90 but still needs stabilisers. Suspension lock-outs are often used to prevent damage from firing stresses, but have little effect on stability.

The position of the turret will also affect stability, especially when firing across the axis of the chassis: a centrally-mounted turret is best since it will tend to transmit forces down through the centre of the chassis. However, other factors tend to be more important in determining the turret position. A major factor is ammunition replenishment. If an SP gun is expected to fire large quantities of ammunition at a fairly constant rate throughout a day, it will almost certainly have to be resupplied directly from stocks positioned to the rear. This is because using turret stocks and replenishing them involves double handling of ammunition and so takes more time and effort in total. Consequently the breech needs to be as close to the rear of the gun as possible – to minimise the distance across which ammunition has to be passed – and so the turret must be to the rear. Conversely, an SP gun which fires fewer rounds, or fires in bursts with adequate pauses between firing, can use its turret stocks and still have time to replenish them, so the turret can be positioned centrally if desired.

The Russian 2S3 (Figure 5.37) is a good example of this design influence, compared to the M109 or AS90. Although the Russians traditionally use heavy artillery barrages they have relatively large quantities of guns compared to the British Army, for example. Their guns could therefore fire in concentrated bursts and then replenish while other artillery continued the bombardment if necessary. The greater inherent stability due to the central turret allowed the

Figure 5.35 Self-propelled Gun with Limited Top Traverse (US M110)

Figure 5.36 Turreted Self-propelled Gun with Full 6,400 mils Traverse (British AS90)

2S3 to avoid the need for spades. This in itself is an added advantage, since it allows the gun to come into action much faster and thus be more suitable for the rapid advances that are a feature of Russian military doctrine. In this respect, note that the 2S3 weighs about the same as the M109.

SP Guns on Tank Chassis

In recent years, the desire of some nations to save on defence costs has led some to consider building SP guns on old tank chassis. A possible additional advantage is that such a policy can lead to logistic savings through partial commonality of spares between tank and artillery fleets. However, this can lead to design problems for such guns. Most tanks have their power packs in the rear of the chassis, so ammunition cannot be resupplied through this route. Replenishment through the side of the chassis is likely to be prevented by the tracked running gear, and through the front by the desire not to break the integrity of the frontal armour. Consequently, ammunition has to be lifted directly into the turret which will be a human physical problem for medium calibre shells, so some mechanical assistance is necessary. This problem was tackled with automated mechanics in the ill-fated SP70 project undertaken by Britain, Germany and Italy in the 1970s and 80s. Figure 5.38 shows the shell replenishment gear on the rear of the turret of the SP70 (which was mounted on a variation of the Leopard 1 tank chassis) which did not attain adequate

Figure 5.37 Russian 2S3

Figure 5.38 SP70, showing its Shell Replenishment Gear

reliability before the project was halted for this and other reasons. Manually-operated slides are of course more reliable but they require more effort and reduce rates of fire. Modern robotics might provide better solutions, and these are discussed in Chapter 7.

SUMMARY

This chapter has described the several basic components, and the variations in their design, of artillery guns. These can be combined in a wide variety of ways to produce the enormous diversity of gun designs seen in compendia of world-wide equipment. There is no doubt that designs will continue to evolve and that many of the component variations mentioned here will become obsolete, some much sooner than others. However, it is also certain that the vast quantities of equipment built during the Cold War period will remain in service for a considerable period to come, even if not with their original countries of production. Consequently their inclusion here should remain relevant for many years yet.

NOTE

1   G.M. Moss, D.W. Leeming and C.L. Farrar, '*Military Ballistics: A Basic Manual*', Brassey's, London (1995)

6

Rockets

INTRODUCTION

The history of the development of rocket systems has not been as smooth as that of guns and mortars. Until recently many Western armies had primarily, or in some cases exclusively, used rockets only as tactical nuclear delivery vehicles at ranges of around 100km. Other armies, notably those of the Former Soviet Union and Warsaw Pact, had taken a different view, since their principal advantages of range and weight of fire accorded with their philosophy of shock action. Advances in technology eventually provided adequate accuracy and reliability. Consequently, rockets could successfully compete with guns for more of the tasks among the more stringent and financially restricted Western requirements. In particular the ease of obtaining greater range compared to guns made rockets very attractive to meet the requirements of the NATO Follow-On Forces Attack (FOFA), and subsequently the Air–Land Battle concepts of the 1980s and 90s. This led to the development of the Multiple Launch Rocket System (MLRS) in the USA, followed by its production in several European countries, and by the subsequent development of the longer range Army Tactical Missile System (ATACMS) which is also fired from the MLRS launcher. Other advantages of rockets, such as their potential for greater warhead capacity and softer acceleration, make them very suitable as vehicles for dispensing smart submunitions for long-range precision attack.

GENERAL PRINCIPLES

If a gas is held under compression in a closed tube, the pressure is equal on all surfaces (see Figure 6.1). If an opening is present at one end of the tube and the pressure is maintained by burning propellant, the pressure at the closed end will be greater than at the open end. This pressure gradient will cause the gases inside the tube to be expelled from the open end (see Figure 6.2) with a certain velocity.

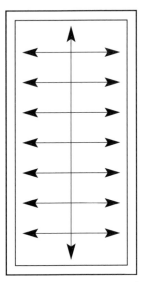

Figure 6.1 Gas Pressure in a Closed Tube

Since the gases now have a velocity in a rearward direction, work must have been done to accelerate them. Newton's Law of equal and opposite reactions indicates that there must be a force acting in the opposite direction on the rocket. This is the thrust on the rocket and is the basic principle upon which it works.

Furthermore, the rocket must conform to the law of conservation of linear momentum, and for any brief period of time this may be expressed as follows:

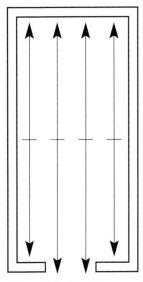

Figure 6.2 Gas Pressure in an Open Tube

Mass of Rocket × Velocity of Rocket = Mass of Gas Expelled × Velocity of Gas

It should be noted that since the mass of the escaping gases will be much less than that of the rocket, the velocity of the rocket will be less than that of the gases. Since the acceleration of the rocket is its rate of change of velocity, it can be calculated from differentiating the above equation as follows:

$$\text{Acceleration} = \frac{\text{Mass of Fuel Consumed per Second} \times \text{Velocity of Gases}}{\text{Mass of Rocket}}$$

From this it can be seen that acceleration is directly proportional to the rate of fuel consumed. Thus if fuel is burnt at a constant rate the acceleration will increase since the mass of the rocket is decreasing (as fuel is burnt). Furthermore, a higher gas velocity will produce a higher acceleration which will in turn give a higher rocket velocity. The gas velocity will depend on the fuel used, the pressure at which it is burnt and on the venting conditions – the conditions under which the gas is expelled from the open end of the rocket. The type of fuel, and in particular its specific energy, is normally the most significant factor.

The formula for calculating the maximum velocity attained by the rocket was derived by Tsiolovsky in 1903. If the effects of gravity and aerodynamic drag are discarded (and they are normally quite small compared to the thrust) this can be stated as:

$$\text{Maximum Velocity} = \frac{\text{Velocity of Gases}^{(i)} \times \text{Log}_e \text{ Initial Mass of Rocket}}{\text{Mass of Rocket when Fuel Consumed}}$$

(i) Note that this is the velocity of gases relative to the rocket, not relative to the surrounding space.

From this it should be noted that the maximum velocity achieved does not depend either on the rate at which fuel is consumed, or on whatever acceleration is experienced. The key factors are the gas velocity and the proportion of fuel by weight in the rocket. It is also significant that the thrust of the rocket is independent of both the velocity of the rocket and also of the atmosphere.

The main components of a free flight rocket (FFR) are the motor, including the combustion chamber and the nozzle, and the warhead, including the fuze. The development of relatively cheap navigational guidance systems is leading to their inclusion in many modern rockets, but such systems should correctly be termed guided weapons, which are considered in Volume I of the 2nd Brassey's Land Warfare Series. However, the distinction is becoming blurred, and some such developments are considered in Chapter 7.

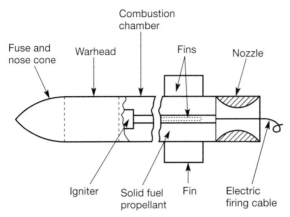

Figure 6.3 Main Components of a Free Flight Rocket

ROCKET MOTORS

Casings

A rocket motor takes up typically two-thirds or more of the total rocket volume. In a solid fuel rocket the casing is effectively the combustion chamber. It is closed at its front end, which is attached to the warhead. A nozzle forms the rear end and there will be an igniter somewhere on the surface of the fuel.

The casing must be geometrically precise in construction and it must be strong enough to withstand the heat and pressure stresses, and therefore not bend during firing, otherwise accuracy and consistency will suffer. Various construction methods have been used, including simple or helically wrapped and welded steel plate, and laminated layers of metal or glass fibre reinforced plastic. Modern methods include cold extrusion which can provide greater strength and precision.

Propellants and Igniters

Now that solid fuelled motors can be made with consistent, reliable performance and since they are simple to use, they are almost always the preferred method for tactical battlefield rockets. Liquid fuelled rocket motors do have several advantages over solid fuelled motors, including better control and power to weight performance, but they have certain disadvantages such as design complexity, cost and long-term storage difficulties. Hence they are generally used for longer range guided weapons, where their higher specific energy, long burning duration and controllability are more important.

Motors can be of the short burning, boost type, or of the longer burning, sustained type. Free flight tactical rockets invariably use boost motors, with burning times typically no more than five seconds, often much less, and with the advantage that the high initial velocity minimises the effect of crosswinds near launch. Boost motors require large burning surfaces, so they are usually hollow, the shape of the cross-section determining the precise rate of burn. The fuel is normally 'platonised' by the addition of lead salts to provide constant burning rates and hence improve performance consistency. The igniter is usually a pyrotechnic compound which is initiated electrically. It must be sited so that it ignites the complete burning surface simultaneously, and this is normally at the front of the motor so that the initial burning motion heads towards the nozzle.

Nozzles

In order to produce the high gas velocity required for maximum thrust, a convergent–divergent nozzle, known as a 'De Laval' nozzle, is normally used. This works on the principle that the mass flow rate of the gas must be constant as it is expelled from the rocket. The nozzle, shown in Figure 6.4, initially increases the gas velocity by constricting the flow area. Then, as the gases emerge into the divergent portion they are expanded to lower temperature and pressure, thus further increasing their velocity. The throat area, exit area and divergent cone angle will primarily determine the gas velocity and therefore the thrust achieved.

The inner slope of the nozzle produces a smooth, non-turbulent flow of gas. The throat must allow sufficient free space for the gases without throttling, but at the same time prevent too rapid an escape so that pressure can be maintained within the rocket. The casing of the rocket motor and the nozzle exert a force on the gases in order to increase their momentum. Newton's Third Law shows that there must be a reaction on the casing and the nozzle, and it is this

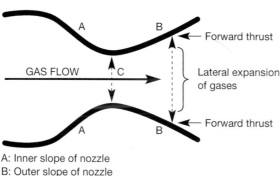

A: Inner slope of nozzle
B: Outer slope of nozzle
C: Throat diameter

Figure 6.4 Critical Dimensions of a Rocket Nozzle

force that is the thrust on the rocket. Typically, 80% of the total thrust is the reaction on the forward end of the motor casing, and 20% is due to the reaction on the nozzle.

The nozzle must be able to withstand the effect of the hot, compressed exhaust gases, if only for a few seconds. This is most critical at the throat. The nozzle material should have a high melting point, good thermal conductivity and be robust enough to withstand the abrasive action of the gases. Metal oxides or carbides, graphite and asbestos components are normally used. Since these can be expensive, they are sometimes used as inserts in the nozzle.

WARHEADS

Due to their limited accuracy, discussed later in this chapter, rockets are primarily designed to attack large areas. The variety of warheads that they can carry reflects this criterion. The simplest warhead is a unitary HE type, and since a rocket experiences far lower accelerations than a shell (typically 50–250g compared to 20,000g) the warhead walls can be designed for optimum fragmentation rather than to withstand firing forces. However, apart from small rockets such as the Russian BM21, unitary HE warheads will only provide sporadic and hence inefficient area coverage. This is a major reason for the design of submunitions such as bomblets and minelets for many modern systems such as the MLRS. These were described briefly in Chapter 2, but are considered further here.

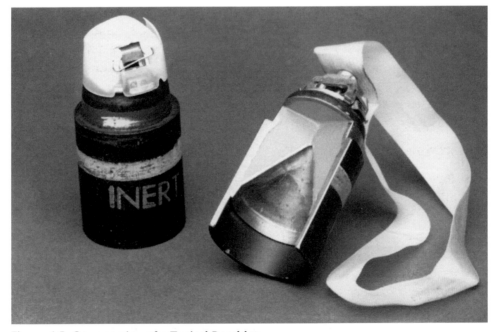

Figure 6.5 Cross-section of a Typical Bomblet

Bomblets

Since rockets generally have large diameters and therefore can have large warhead volumes, designers have considerable scope for varying the sizes of submunitions to be carried. For a given warhead volume, if bomblets are large there will be fewer of them but they will have a better effect if they hit; if they are small there will be more of them, giving a higher hit probability, but less destruction from each one. The designer's task, given a range of typical targets, will be to determine the optimum bomblet size. A single MLRS rocket contains 644 bomblets, so when a complete 12 rocket load is fired 7,728 bomblets are deposited on the target area which may typically be up to 1km square – nearly one in every 10 metre square. This bomblet, similar to the one shown in Figure 6.5, has both a fragmentation effect and an armour piercing effect. The fragmentation ensures a good coverage capability against personnel and light vehicles, while the HEAT warhead provides good penetration if the bomblet hits the top of a lightly armoured vehicle.

Minelets

Another advantage of the low acceleration of rockets is that components of submunitions are subjected to less force on firing. Consequently delicate electronic circuits and mechanisms can be used more easily than in shells. Some rockets are now being designed to carry small mines which are ejected above the target area and fall to the ground under a parachute. The natural inconsistency of the dispersion system ensures a reasonably even coverage of the target with the minelets. Electronic circuits inside the minelet can provide both intelligent fuzing – to improve the kill rate – and also a variable-time self-destruct mechanism to ensure that the minefield, which cannot be plotted accurately, does not subsequently hinder the movement of friendly forces.

Smart Sub-munitions

The lower acceleration of a rocket also makes it easier to construct 'smart' submunitions which can be terminally aimed (with fixed radar or infra-red sensors), or terminally guided (with delicate seeker, control and guidance mechanisms). These devices, deployed from rockets once near the target area, can engage point targets including armour. They have been successfully developed, but not yet produced, for Phase III of the MLRS. Each Phase III rocket contains three submunitions which, once dispensed, would search for a suitable target using millimetric radar, home onto it and attack from the top with a shaped charge HEAT warhead. This and similar systems are described further in Chapter 7.

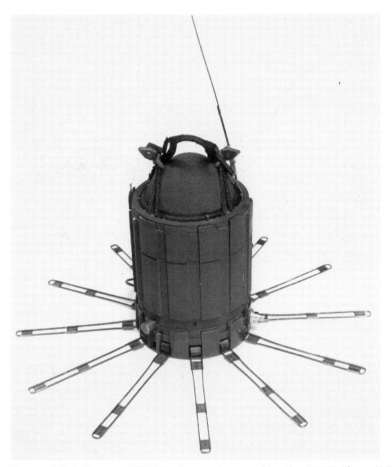

Figure 6.6 A German AT2 Minelet as dispersed by the MLRS Phase II Rocket

Other Warheads

Rockets have been designed since the end of World War II by certain countries to carry nuclear and chemical warheads. Once again, their large capacity and low launch force make them well suited for such devices.

STABILISATION

Spin or fin stabilisation, or both, can be used for rockets. Spin stabilisation minimises the effect of any thrust misalignment in the rocket motor while it is firing, the implications of which are discussed later. Spin can be imparted either as the rocket leaves the launcher by using helical guides in the launch tube, or by angling the motor nozzles to give a rotational effect. The necessary rate of spin increases with the length to diameter ratio of a projectile. Rockets

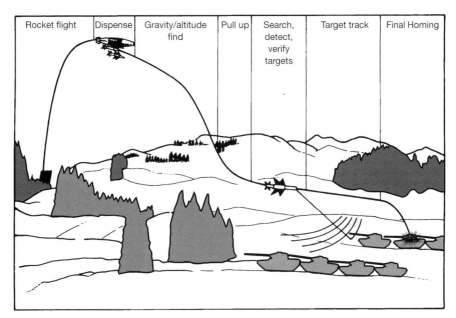

Rocket flight	Dispense	Gravity/altitude find	Pull up	Search, detect, verify targets	Target track	Final Homing

Figure 6.7 Schematic for a Terminally Guided Submunition

tend to be long and thin for optimum aerodynamic flight, so spin rates need to be very high, which can be difficult to achieve from a short launch tube.

Fins increase the susceptibility of the rocket to crosswind effects so they should be kept as small as possible. Conversely, they need to be large in order to provide adequate stability to overcome the problem of motor thrust misalignment. Modern rockets, such as MLRS, now tend to use a combination of fin and spin stabilisation in order to achieve optimum effects while maintaining accuracy.

ACCURACY

The principal disadvantage of rockets is their relatively poor accuracy and consistency compared to guns. This increases significantly with range: a rocket launcher may need to fire twice or even three times as many rockets at maximum range compared to mid-range in order to achieve similar effects on a target of given size.

Thrust Misalignment

Unlike a gun, the thrust on a rocket continues to be applied after it has left the guiding effect of the launch rail or tube. If the direction of rocket motor thrust does not pass through the centre of gravity of the rocket, the misalignment will cause potentially large errors in line at the target unless the rocket is spun.

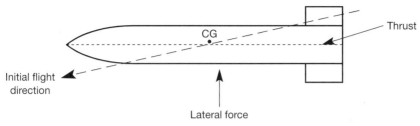

Note: Rocket will rotate clockwise. CG = centre of gravity
Figure 6.8 Thrust Misalignment

It is very difficult and expensive to manufacture perfectly both a motor and the other components of a rocket in order to avoid thrust misalignment. The propellant must be positioned centrally, and the nozzle axis, the gas efflux axis and the rocket casing must all be symmetrical. It is also possible for the casing to bend under the high internal pressures or if there is asymmetrical heating from the motor. If thrust misalignment occurs, the rocket will tend to rotate and yaw, as shown in Figure 6.8. As already mentioned, this effect can be at least partially overcome by spinning the rocket. A very short motor burning time can also assist, since this will reduce the time outside the launch tube when thrust misalignment will have an effect. Motor burning times of one to four seconds are common. However, the shorter burning time will impose higher acceleration forces on the structure, which will demand a more robust and heavier casing, to the detriment of maximum range or warhead capacity.

Crosswind Effects

Compared to shells, the large longitudinal cross-section of rockets – especially those with large fins – makes them susceptible to crosswinds. The effect is to turn the nose of the rocket into the wind, since the wind will act mainly on the fins which are at the rear. It will be greatest when the rocket velocity is low, and this will therefore occur immediately after launch. For the same reason the effect will also be greater on rockets with low acceleration, so motors with short burning times are desirable, just as they are to minimise the effects of thrust misalignment. It is obviously desirable to minimise the size of the fins, but a balance must be struck between smaller fins and the larger fins needed for better stability. As discussed earlier when considering stability, fin size can be reduced if the rocket is spun. Spin-stabilised rockets without fins will also be affected by crosswinds, to about the same extent or slightly less than a similar sized rocket with both fin and spin stabilisation.

Velocity at All-burnt

Because of aerodynamic effects, notably drag, the fuel burning rate can make a significant difference to the velocity of the rocket when 'all-burnt' occurs, which in turn will affect the range achieved. Careful manufacture of the fuel can yield more consistent burning, as can 'platonisation' – the addition of lead salts – which was mentioned earlier in this chapter. However, the burning rate is also affected by temperature and pressure: it will increase as they increase. Rockets will normally have specified temperatures and pressures outside which their performance will be erratic, leading to inaccuracy and inconsistency at the target.

Launcher Induced Errors

The launcher will move slightly as a rocket is fired, since there will be some reaction to the movement and weight of the rocket as it travels along the rail or launch tube. This is particularly significant when firing a salvo from a multiple launch system. The problem can be overcome to some extent by using stabilising legs and/or spades, or automatic control systems with inertial sensors, but there will inevitably need to be a short time delay between rocket firings to maintain accuracy and consistency. Such components will come with financial and possibly weight penalties, and are usually only justified for larger, long-range systems.

A further problem can be the difficulty in ensuring that the shoes or lugs holding the rocket to its rails or within its tube release simultaneously. If they do not, a 'tip-off' effect will occur when the forward part of the rocket is unsupported as it clears the rail or tube and will tend to tip downwards. Modern design and manufacturing seem to have solved this problem.

RANGE COVERAGE

Minimum Range

Since a solid fuelled rocket has only one 'charge', range can normally be altered only through changing the launch elevation. This means that for short ranges the elevation would be very low and crest clearances over intervening high ground are likely to prevent operation. A possible means of reducing range is to use air brakes to increase drag. Even with such brakes, however, a rocket, unless it has a very small calibre, will rarely have a viable range of less than 10km, but this may not restrict firing unduly since launchers are normally deployed many kilometres to the rear of forward troops for survivability. Furthermore, they tend not to be used for very close support due to their inaccuracy and large safety distance, which may be over 2km for a system like the MLRS firing bomblet warheads.

Maximum Range

The maximum range of a given size of rocket can only be increased, during design, by varying the ratio of fuel weight and volume to that of the warhead. For longer ranges the warhead must therefore be smaller and/or lighter. For the MLRS, this allows the Phase II minelet rocket, which weighs considerably less than the Phase I version, to have maximum range some 7km greater than that of the Phase I bomblet rocket. Alternatively, the MLRS Extended Range rocket will have a range of around 50km, compared to 30km, but it will only carry about two-thirds of the number of bomblets. An alternative approach to increasing the range significantly while retaining a large warhead is to design a larger rocket to be fired from the same launcher. Hence the ATACMS has been developed with a range of over 150km and can be fired from an MLRS launcher, although it takes up the space of one rocket pod container (RPC) which would normally contain six Phase I or Phase II rockets.

LAUNCHERS

Launchers provide a means of supporting and aiming the rocket. They can have single or multiple rails or tubes, although modern practice is almost exclusively to use a multiple launch capability. Only very large rockets are normally launched singly, but since these tend to have some form of guidance they are not technically FFRs but guided missiles instead. Another reason for having a multiple capability is that the rocket exhaust exhibits a very large firing signature, so there is a need to maximise the number of warheads fired in a short burst, after which the launcher moves from the firing point. Tubes are generally favoured over rails in order to protect the rocket against shell splinters and damage in transit and to allow spin to be imparted to the rocket without the need for extra thrusters.

Since a rocket moves forward by ejecting gases rather than by a reaction with a barrel, a rocket launcher does not need a recoil mechanism nor does it have to withstand significant firing stresses. It can therefore be both mechanically simpler and also lighter than a gun. In fact there are reactions due to both friction on the rail or tube and also the effect of exhaust gases hitting the launcher body, but these are relatively small. Together they can have two effects: firstly, they will rock the launcher enough to require a delay of a few seconds before firing the next rocket if accuracy is to be maintained; secondly, the gas efflux can be corrosive, so panels of protective material – sometimes known as 'ablative panels' – may have to be fixed to the launcher.

The lack of launcher reaction, or trunnion pull, also means that an increase in range does not require an increase in the weight of the launcher. It only

Figure 6.9 A Rail Launcher (Honest John)

needs to be as heavy and strongly constructed as is necessary to support and, usually, to transport the rocket load. For example, an MLRS launcher fires a Phase I rocket weighing over 300kg to a range of 30km, yet it weighs the same as an M109 gun which only fires a 43kg shell to 24km.

Launch Length

A launcher can have no effective length of rail – a 'zero length' launcher – or it can have 'positive length'. With zero length, the rocket is free from the rail as soon as it begins to move, so consequently the rail simply acts as a support to point the rocket in the right direction. Whilst they have the advantage of being short, such systems are only likely to be used for guided weapons, where post-launch control is exerted on the flight of the rocket.

The 'positive length' rail or tube is a compromise between two prime factors. A long rail will maintain the rocket in the desired direction for a longer time during launch and thus provide extra guidance and accuracy, but the rail must be supported and be strong enough not to bend as the rocket travels down it, and this will increase its weight. Alternatively, a short rail is less likely to affect the dimensions and weight of the complete launcher, which will normally be required to be as small and as light as possible for tactical and mobility reasons.

Figure 6.10 Multiple Launch Rocket System (MLRS)

If the rocket can accelerate quickly towards maximum velocity while it is still on the rail or in the tube then accuracy will be improved. This is therefore yet another reason, in addition to those mentioned earlier in this chapter, for having a motor with a short burning time.

Launcher Design

Modern multiple launchers tend to be designed in one of two ways. They can be very basic, using optical sighting and manual loading and aiming. The simplest can be very small, light and comparable to medium mortars yet have a greater initial target effect. Modern examples include the South African Mechem RO68 and RO107. The RO68 is a four-tube launcher weighing 33kg, which fires 4 × 6.8kg rockets in five seconds to a maximum range of nearly 2.5km. The system can be carried by two men and is primarily designed for special force operations. The RO107 launcher has 12 × 107mm tubes, weighs 385kg and is normally towed, although it can be broken down into 30kg loads for manportability. It can be brought into action in ten minutes, fire 12 × 19kg rockets in nine seconds to a maximum range of 8.5km, and then be brought out of action in five minutes.

Rather more complex are launchers such as the Russian BM21, the Italian FIROS 6 and FIROS 25, and the German Light Artillery Rocket System (LARS). These are simple to operate and maintain yet provide a reasonably high level of firepower in a short time. For example, the BM21 fires up to 36×120mm rockets in 18 seconds. However, they are relatively slow into action, requiring external orientation, and will also take some time to reload and move. They are well suited to use by conscript armies, where there is comparatively little time for the training of both operators and maintainers. Like most rocket systems, their capability can be enhanced by improvements to the warhead, perhaps by including bomblets, minelets or terminally guided weapons, without any significant training burden.

A similar type of system, but rather more versatile, is the Brazilian ASTROS. This is optically orientated for firing but it can accommodate a variety of rocket calibres. As shown in Figure 6.12, ASTROS contains four boxes inside which are the launcher tubes. Each box, which requires mechanical assistance for removal and replacement, can contain three calibres of rocket: 8×127mm rockets with a maximum range of 30km, 4×180mm rockets with a maximum range of 35km or one 300mm rocket with a maximum range of 60km.

Figure 6.11 BM21

Fig 6.12 ASTROS
Note the Mount for the Optical Dial Sight (centre rear of the tubes) and the Rocket
Pod Containers

More advanced systems, such as the MLRS, have a large number of electronic and mechanical systems on board to provide considerable automation. MLRS was originally designed in the United States and is also fielded in several other NATO countries including Britain, Germany and France. Subsequent developments have been both national and multinational, although commonality and interchangeability are maintained as far as possible. Each launcher has an orientation and distance measurement system which provides an instantaneous indication of location and bearing. It also has a ballistic firing computer, which will calculate the firing data and feed this to the traverse and elevation motors. The motors can then automatically point the rockets on the correct bearing and elevation. The launcher also has an assisted loading mechanism which, operated by one man if necessary, can reload two pods each of 6 × 227mm rockets in about two minutes. These various systems allow the crew of three to fire one set of rockets containing nearly 8,000 bomblets in under one minute, move several kilometres to a reload point and then to a new firing point and fire again, all in under 15 minutes. The latest version of the same launcher could alternatively reload and fire two ATACMS rockets, to a range of around 150km, in a similar timeframe.

Figure 6.13 Army Tactical Missile System (ATACMS)

SUMMARY

As described in Chapter 3 when comparing indirect fire launchers, FFRs provide an efficient means of delivering massive firepower in a short time at long range, often from comparatively simple, light equipment. They normally have considerable scope for including a wide range of warheads, especially those with advanced electronic seekers for precision attack. Some launcher designs are also well suited to firing a variety of rockets with different maximum ranges without any need for modification. Furthermore, low cost electronic navigation systems can be included to make significant improvements to accuracy. They are thus very versatile and despite their logistic penalties they seem certain to maintain, and possibly increase, their importance as a major force component in most armies in the future.

NOTE

1. R.G. Lee *et al.*, *'Guided Weapons'*, Brassey's, London (1988)

7

Future Trends

FUTURE REQUIREMENTS

In the future it seems likely that indirect fire will continue to be used in two types of conflict: operations of high intensity, such as the Gulf War, and lower level intervention operations primarily involving peacemaking. Limited defence expenditure and smaller forces mean that the same equipment may have to be used in both types of conflict. However, the often conflicting demands of strategic and tactical mobility will provide a strong reason for maintaining both armoured, heavy systems for high intensity conflict and lightweight systems where rapid strategic deployment and operational redeployment are required.

Certain characteristics of future conflicts are likely to provide the major determining factors for trends in indirect fire design:

The 'extended' or 'less dense' battlefield, referring to smaller armies and the greater dispersion of their formations than was likely in NATO Central Region scenarios, is already leading to demands for greater range.

The requirement to retain public support, both internationally (through the United Nations) and nationally, will lead to strong arguments to minimise casualties amongst own troops, civilians and the enemy as well. Furthermore, there will often be pressure to minimise collateral damage to the environment. In turn, these will require precision targeting and high terminal accuracy. Public awareness of these possibilities has been derived, for example, from television images of missiles flying down city streets to destroy specific buildings in Baghdad during the Gulf War. Consequently the knowledge that technology now exists to provide such accuracy strengthens the argument for precision, notwithstanding the fact that a 'smart' munition is still much more expensive than many so-called 'dumb' munitions.

These same requirements for minimum damage may also encourage the development of Non-Lethal Weapons (NLW) which only disable rather than physically destroy equipment or its operators. This is an area where ethical issues are hotly debated. A lack of knowledge and misunderstanding about NLW often generate fierce arguments about their utility and practicality, and this is further complicated by the possibility that many weapons designed to be non-lethal can be lethal in certain circumstances.

The use of technology to reduce the manning requirement for new equipment, a process which is already under way, will continue. Although the initial capital costs of complex equipment can be high, the long-term running costs are usually significantly less than the costs of training and supporting large numbers of soldiers.

Finally, with western European nations becoming more prepared to operate outside NATO's former Central Region (mainly Germany), the importance of strategic mobility will increase. This will lead to the need for lighter weapon platforms. It should be remembered, however, that in normal circumstances the weight of a mortar, gun or rocket launcher is much less than that of the total quantity of ammunition that it will be expected to fire. Moreover, if deployment is by ship then volume rather than weight is often the determining factor in how much equipment can be carried and hence how quickly a force can be deployed.

Methods of meeting these requirements, and other potential developments, are discussed in this chapter.

SYSTEM IMPROVEMENTS

The importance of viewing mortars, guns and rockets as part of an indirect fire system was stressed and illustrated in Chapter 2. Therefore, although other volumes in this series deal with developments in target acquisition, C^4I and munitions, certain necessary and complementary improvements to other elements of the indirect fire system need to be mentioned here.

Target Acquisition

Most of the problems of target location have been solved for forward observers, operating in close support of armoured and infantry units, by the use of inertial navigation and the Global Positioning System together with laser range finders and battlefield radars. These initially provide a precise location for the observer and then, by determining an accurate bearing and range to the target, they allow an accurate target location to be computed. For depth fire against targets out of visual range from front line troops a wide range of location systems continue to be developed. These include Remotely Piloted Vehicles (RPVs), drones and airborne stand-off radars, which can provide instantaneous transmission of target data and images. Other sources include weapon locating radars which detect mortar bombs, shells and rockets in flight. Examples of such systems include the US Joint Surveillance and Target Attack System (JSTARS) and the UK Airborne Stand-Off Radar (ASTOR), the Israeli RPV Pioneer, the UK RPV Phoenix, and Weapon Locating Radar such as the US Firefinder and the European Cobra. Such systems have only become possible because of the dramatic improvement in computing power available, largely due to developments in the civilian market.

Command, Control, Communications and Computation (C^4)

Many countries have made use of computing technologies to improve their ability to command and control artillery. The UK's Battlefield Artillery Target Engagement System (BATES) is a good example of a system which provides significant enhancements to all elements of C^4 and Intelligence. It is programmed to take account of considerable amounts of information about firing units (such as location and ammunition stocks) and about targets (such as type, size and location) and future plans. According to priorities set by commanders the computer processors can then suggest which firing units should engage which targets to provide the most effective response on a complex battlefield, and it will of course provide the necessary ballistic computation. Commanders have the option of making this process automatic, so that once an observer has entered target data the system will select the most suitable firing units and send their guns the relevant ballistic data. Many other functions are also available, such as automatic prompting of the need to resupply firing units with ammunition since it will keep a record of how much each one has fired.

There are likely to be several advantages in moving ballistic computation from a command post, where it is presently carried out, to each gun. This is already provided on advanced rocket systems such as the MLRS. Such on-board computation would allow guns to operate almost autonomously, improving their freedom of movement and thus their survivability. It should also provide better accuracy since it would allow detailed data on muzzle velocity and charge temperature variations to be accounted for almost instantaneously.

Meteorology

There are two main reasons for the inaccuracy of met prediction: the remoteness of the weapon platform from the met station (typically up to 35km); and the inability to provide 'down range' met, i.e. met conditions throughout the trajectory of the weapon. More local met can be provided by deploying several of the compact stations which are now available. The Vaisala system can be deployed in just two Land Rovers with a crew of four operators, compared to older systems which are fitted in several large lorries and need around 20 men to operate them. The procurement of modern systems on a scale of one for each regiment of guns and each battery of MLRS would reduce the distance between the met station and the weapon platform to a few kilometres.

Methods to solve the 'down range' problem effectively are being investigated. One possible solution is to use remote sensing whereby interpretation of the reflections from the atmosphere of a low powered laser over distances of tens of kilometres can indicate wind speeds and directions. Another concept is to use micro-forecasting, where atmospheric conditions are predicted in much the same way as for national weather forecasts but in much finer detail using both strategic met sources and local information such as the network of military tactical met stations described above.

Logistics

A major requirement for future forces will be to reduce their logistic burden. This is especially important for rapid deployment forces, for which artillery ammunition normally represents the major logistic constraint to movement and, possibly, to operations. For propellant, the key is to make it more kinetically efficient so that less volume and weight of charge are required to achieve a given range. Possible methods of doing this are described later in this chapter. Another solution is to avoid wastage of propellant. At present when firing low charges the unwanted propellant bags are destroyed since they are not interchangeable. If all the charge increments in a cartridge are made of the same size, those not required for shorter range fire missions need not be discarded but can be used to build up cartridges for future missions. This is the concept behind the Modular Charge System (MCS), which is designed for use in future guns of several NATO nations.

The quantity of shells and rockets could be reduced by making their warheads more effective in order to achieve a given target effect. This can be achieved by improving accuracy of delivery, which is discussed later, or by the employment of precision weapons. The latter can be either terminally guided or terminally aimed, and are likely to present considerable advantages both operationally and logistically. However, their use may require careful control since if they are very effective they may result in extra fire missions being conducted. Thus the total quantity of precision ammunition used may be less than that of 'dumb' munitions needed to achieve the same effect in a complete operation, although for short periods the number of rounds required may be just as high. Consequently the strategic burden would be reduced, but the tactical resupply limitations would remain.

LONG RANGE

Longer Barrels

Increased range can be provided by using longer barrels, thus increasing the time for which work is being done on the projectile. For example, a 52 calibre (eight metre) barrel is available to be fitted to the AS90, replacing the original 39 calibre (six metre) barrel. However, lengthening the barrel of a gun needs to be accompanied by a larger chamber volume if the full benefits are to be obtained, and so the 52 calibre barrel fitted to both the AS90 and the German PHz 2000 has an increased chamber volume of 23 litres, the combination being designed to comply with the revised NATO Joint Ballistics Memorandum Of Understanding (MOU). This MOU seeks to achieve commonality of internal ballistics in guns and thus interoperability of ammunition systems between the signatory nations. It should be noted however that there are limitations and disadvantages to longer barrels, especially for guns. Obviously a long barrel may cause mobility problems by increasing the length of the gun or mortar. It is also likely to weigh more and to make the ordnance more out of balance, so a stronger, heavier recoil mechanism – to absorb the recoil energy – and stronger balancing gear may both be required. Finally, a longer barrel is more prone to causing vibration as the shell travels down the bore, which in turn can affect ballistics and wear on both the bore and the shell.

ALTERNATIVE GUN PROPELLANTS

One obvious solution to the requirement to increase the range of a given weight of shell is to launch it with greater muzzle velocity. In turn, this may require a greater energy input from the charge, and so considerable research and development effort continues in order to develop practical propellants with a higher specific energy (energy per unit mass). Increases in the specific energy of solid propellants are quite possible but this may lead to increased barrel stresses and to a higher flame temperature, which in turn can make ignition more difficult unless special additives are included. An additional consideration is that if smart, precision-attack shells containing sensitive electronic components are to be fired then there will be a need to launch them with lower accelerations so that the delicate sensors survive the forces at launch.

Liquid Propellants

The use of liquid propellant (LP) has been investigated since the end of the Second World War. Initially, bulk-loaded prototypes were developed in which the LP was injected into a simple chamber and then ignited. Sometimes a bi-propellant design was used in which two separate liquids were mixed together in the chamber, the advantage being that one or both were relatively inert until they were mixed together. A schematic diagram of a bulk-loaded LP gun is shown in Figure 7.1. There are two major problems with such a system. Firstly, unless the chamber is full the presence of a void can affect ignition and burning, depending on the elevation of the barrel. Secondly, the LP will need to be pumped fast in order to achieve a high rate of fire and this will tend to create air bubbles which lead to detonation and inconsistent burning.

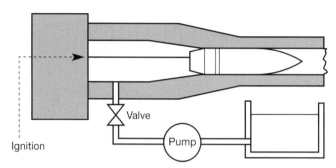

Figure 7.1 A Bulk Loaded Mono-liquid Propellant Gun

More recent designs have used a single propellant and a regenerative ignition system as shown in Figure 7.2. Here, once the shell has been loaded, the liquid is injected into a space between two pistons, the control piston and the injector piston, moving them apart until the required quantity has been metered. A small quantity of liquid is bled into the space between the shell and the pistons and is then ignited. The resulting pressure moves the control piston back, forcing more liquid into the chamber. Both pistons then move backwards, automatically maintaining the required injection rate by virtue of their relative cross-sectional areas: if the chamber pressure increases too rapidly the injector piston moves back faster, thereby closing the annular orifice between the two piston heads and reducing the propellant injection rate.

LP has several significant advantages over solid propellants. It is cheap to manufacture, perhaps being 25% cheaper than solid propellants. It has a higher energy density and can provide a better piezometric efficiency (i.e. lower peak pressure), so less propellant needs to be carried for a given number of rounds fired and lower accelerations can be achieved, allowing smart shells to be used with more delicate components such as sensors. The bulk movement and storage of LP is easier and it can be loaded automatically and fast, allowing high rates of fire. Furthermore, it offers the potential for an infinite variation of charge rather than the discrete steps of a solid cartridge system. In turn, this means that several rounds can be fired at different muzzle velocities (and possibly different elevations) which can allow the simultaneous impact on a single target of perhaps six shells from one gun, achieving tremendous shock effect.

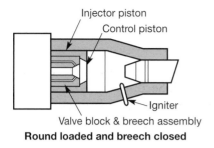

Injector piston
Control piston

Igniter

Valve block & breech assembly

Round loaded and breech closed

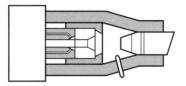

Propellant injected

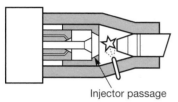

Injector passage

Ignition - control piston starts to move
back, the annular injector passage
opens pressuring the propellant
which begins to enter the chamber.

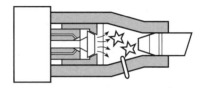

Control and injector pistons move
back together automatically
maintaining the designed propellant
delivery rate. Round starts to move.

Figure 7.2 A Regenerative Mono-liquid Propellant Gun

However, LP does have significant developmental problems. It requires a relatively complex handling system, including a high performance valve and other seals which can withstand the high breech pressures generated. The breech for an LP gun is also likely to be larger and more complex than that for solid propellants, and the LP can be both corrosive and toxic. Finally, the current ability of LP guns to provide repeatable muzzle velocities is doubtful.

The potential advantages of LP are so attractive that the concept was investigated by the US for several years in their Defender research programme and was for a period the preferred solution for their Crusader Advanced Field Artillery System (AFAS), due into service early in the 21st century. The 155mm Defender gun has achieved muzzle velocities of over 1,000 m/s and ranges of 4.5 to 45km, which compares very well with the best solid propellant guns. The combination of LP and automated ammunition handling (discussed later) were intended to allow a rate of fire of 10 to 12 rounds per minute to be achieved.

Electro-Thermal Guns

Electro-Thermal (ET) guns all work on the basis of using electrical energy to modify the internal ballistic cycle of a relatively conventional ordnance. The energy is used to maximise the efficiency of the gun. There is, however, a wide variety of concepts under research and development, some of which appear to be more promising than others.

The simplest type is often referred to as a 'pure ET' gun: here electrical energy in the form of a plasma discharge is used to heat a working medium such as water which absorbs heat. In doing so it vaporises, thereby pressurising the chamber in much the same way as a solid propellant does when it burns. However, by varying the electrical input the pressure-time curve can in turn be altered and hence projectile acceleration and muzzle velocity can be controlled. The attraction of such a system is that inert, and probably cheap, working fluids can be used, but the prime disadvantage appears to be that a considerable quantity of electrical energy is required in each pulse and these would be difficult to generate in a sustained manner.

An alternative and currently more promising system is Electro-Thermal-Chemical (ETC) propulsion. Here, the electrical energy is again used to generate a plasma discharge but this now acts on an exothermic working medium – a propellant which generates heat as a result of this initiation process. Plasma is very hot and light so it will ignite the propellant evenly and rapidly, even if the latter is relatively dense. Furthermore, the rate of propellant combustion can be controlled by varying the electrical input, which in turn will control the pressure driving the projectile and hence its muzzle velocity.

A significant advantage of ETC technology is that it could be used with existing solid propellant guns. A diagram of such a system is at Figure 7.3.

This shows a modified breech which generates the plasma jet when electrical energy is applied. The jet is firstly used to ignite the solid propellant somewhat faster than the current primer would do, and then to modify the burn rate. This would not only increase the muzzle velocity whilst reducing peak acceleration, but by measuring bore pressure and feeding this data back to the electrical control system it could also be used to control the muzzle velocity and thereby increase accuracy. The effect of doing this would produce a pressure-space curve of the form suggested in Figure 7.4.

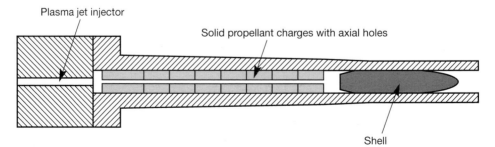

Figure 7.3 Electro-Thermal-Chemical Gun Concept using Solid Propellant

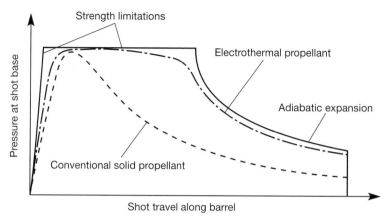

Figure 7.4 Pressure-Space Curve for an Electro-Thermal Gun

Electromagnetic Guns

The use of electromagnetic (EM) energy to launch projectiles has been under research for some time. Various concepts have been considered, but the basic principle for all of them is that a large quantity of electrical energy is discharged into rails or coils which form the 'barrel' of the gun. This sets up a powerful magnetic field which, by acting on an armature at the rear of the projectile, accelerates it to extremely high velocity – at least 2,000 m/s. At present such guns can only operate with relatively light projectiles, and the problem of storing sufficient electrical energy for, say, five rounds to be fired has yet to be solved practically. Assuming that the various problems can be solved, their prime application, at least in the medium term, is therefore seen to be as direct fire weapons where requirements are for a high energy density in the projectile and not for sustained fire of heavy shells.

FUTURE LONG-RANGE MUNITIONS

Shell Modifications

Various methods of extending the firing range of shells by modifying them directly have been discussed in Chapter 3. One further method of increasing range which is being considered is the fitting of a ram jet into a shell. This would take up more space than a base bleed unit, but perhaps not as much as a rocket, and might give even better range improvements than either. It should be remembered, however, that the inconsistencies in the jet and most of the previously mentioned shell modifications are likely to degrade accuracy.

Rocket Modifications

Extending the range of rockets by the use of more propellant has already been mentioned in Chapter 6. Perhaps the best example is the MLRS/ATACMS combination, where the initial 32km range of MLRS Phase I will shortly be increased to over 300km for ATACMS Block II. Alternatively, like the shell discussed above, a rocket could also use a ram jet, and compared to its use in shells the relative loss of payload may not be so great. However, once again in order to retain acceptable target effects some means of improving accuracy would almost certainly have to be incorporated.

INCREASED ACCURACY

As discussed earlier in this chapter, improvements in accuracy, especially at the much longer ranges now possible, would reduce the quantity of ammunition needed for a given task and hence reduce the logistic problem of moving it to the launcher.

Establishing the location of the weapon platform has been significantly improved by the use of inertial navigators. These can be fitted either in survey vehicles or directly into the platforms themselves, such as AS90 and MLRS. When combined with the use of GPS to provide world-wide coverage, platform location should be adequate for all requirements.

Firing Data

The most significant remaining problems in producing more accurate firing data for guns are meteorological prediction (discussed earlier in this chapter) and muzzle velocity (MV) prediction. Extensive measurements have shown that MV prediction is very difficult to achieve, since there appears to be a high degree of randomness even when the same charge is being fired constantly. However, the development of algorithms to predict MVs is being pursued and recent results using advanced knowledge-based computers and programs which 'learn' appear very promising. They do need to know the MV of every round fired, which is why all guns in UK service, for example, are now fitted with an instantaneous MV measuring device.

With the trend to the use of long barrels in order to achieve very long ranges, there is a possible need for a muzzle reference system, as already used on tank guns. A 52 calibre 155mm barrel, about eight metres long, is liable to bend by several mils when it is hot and is being unevenly cooled by air movement. Using a laser reflected back from a mirror mounted above the muzzle would allow this deviation to be measured and incorporated in firing data.

Various other errors, while relatively small compared to met and MV variations, are likely to have a significant cumulative effect at very long ranges. The measurement of variations in shell weight, chamber temperature and charge temperature is possible, but transmitting the data from the gun to the battery computer before firing data are computed would probably take too long. The obvious solution, as mentioned earlier in this Chapter, is to provide ballistic computation on board the gun itself, and this is certainly feasible if the size and cost of computers reduce at the current rate.

Terminal Guidance

Despite the above advances, indirect fire using simple ballistics will never achieve adequate accuracy to engage point targets. To do so successfully requires terminal guidance in the weapon. Inertial guidance or GPS could be fitted into shells and rockets, allowing them to home autonomously onto the programmed target location. In shells such systems would need to be very rugged and they would be costly. However, relatively cheap guidance systems for future MLRS long-range rockets are likely to be fielded in the early 21st century. Complete trajectory adjustment for a shell or rocket would effectively require it to become a guided missile with control systems such as fins.

A simpler solution for a shell is based on the fact that errors in range are far greater than those for line. Consequently, rather than provide full guidance for the shell, which would require considerable space to be devoted to control mechanisms, a simple air brake is provided to limit range. The shell is deliberately fired so that it would over-range the target and the position sensor deploys the air brake at the precise time needed to land the shell on the target. A ten-fold improvement in accuracy at ranges in excess of 30km has been suggested by studies into this concept. This is likely to be adequate provided that the target is a small area rather than a point such as an armoured vehicle.

Laser-guided Shells

Semi-autonomous guided shells have already been fielded by both the US (with Copperhead) and Russia (various versions of Krasnopol). These use laser seekers to home in on light reflected from a point target illuminated by a hand-held or remotely operated laser target marker (LTM). However, the shells are much longer than standard shells of the same calibre and consequently present handling difficulties. Their use requires close control to ensure that the LTM is switched on at the correct time and its beam is maintained on the target, and they may not be able to lock onto the laser reflection from the target in poor weather conditions.

Autonomous Munitions

Autonomous indirect fire weapons which are terminally aimed or guided have been under development for many years. These only require approximate target locations and no external target illumination. Terminally aimed munitions are sometimes referred to as Sensor Fused Munitions. They include the US Sense and Destroy Armour (SADARM) submunition, which could be fitted inside a shell or a rocket, the Russian MOTIV-3M submunition which is designed for their Smerch 300mm MRL, and the German Smart 155 and French/Swedish Bonus, both designed for 155mm shells. They use a fixed millimetric wave seeker or a fixed infra-red seeker or a combination of both, which search in a spiral pattern generated by an off-centre parachute or wings deployed in the last few seconds of the weapon's flight. Once the seeker has found a target it initiates a self-forging fragment warhead for top-attack. The fact that there are very few moving parts in these munitions makes them more resilient to forces generated by high accelerations and hence it is now possible to launch them from a gun.

Since a mortar provides lower launch accelerations it can use weapons with more moving parts. The British Aerospace Merlin 81mm mortar bomb uses a millimetric wave radar seeker controlling fins which guide it onto the target, which it attacks with a HEAT warhead. Both classes of weapons exploit the fact that the top armour of all AFVs is relatively thin. However, their calibre or

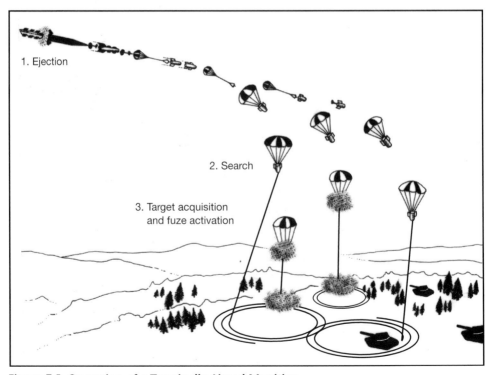

Figure 7.5 Operation of a Terminally Aimed Munition

attack mechanism may give inadequate penetration if complex armours are fitted to the top of their potential targets.

MLRS Autonomous Warheads

One of the most promising autonomous weapon developments in recent years has been the MLRS Terminally Guided Warhead system. A variant of the 227mm diameter rocket is designed to carry three terminally guided submunitions (TGSMs). These are deployed near the target area and search for armoured vehicles using a scanning millimetric radar which provides information to guide them onto the target, attacking it with a powerful shaped charge warhead on contact. Successful tests of the system have been carried out but for various reasons, primarily financial, three of the original four collaborators – the US, UK and Germany – have dropped out of the programme leaving only France to continue development.

Another MLRS-launched autonomous system is the Brilliant Anti-Tank (BAT) warhead. This is designed to be deployed from the larger, longer range ATACMS rocket. A development model is pictured in Figure 7.5. It uses a combination of an acoustic sensor for coarse sensing of a target and then final guidance is provided from a millimetric wave radar seeker. Such a system

Figure 7.6 The Brilliant Anti-Tank (BAT) Submunition

would provide precision attack of individual targets at over 300km range and could revolutionise the way in which land-based weapons are used to fight battles, by destroying key targets and even large armoured concentrations long before they are engaged in a contact battle with opposing tanks.

Fibre-optic Guided Missiles

The ultimate in long-range accuracy would be achieved by guiding a rocket throughout its flight and onto a specific target. This is now becoming possible with the development of long-range fibre-optic guided missiles (FOGM) such as the E-FOGM from the US and Polyphem from Germany and France. This concept uses a small TV camera in the nose of a missile which transmits its picture down a fibre-optic cable which is dispensed behind it in flight. The picture is viewed by the weapon controller who, for improved survivability, is unlikely to be in direct line of sight to the target; this is therefore a form of indirect fire system. The controller can guide the missile constantly, or alternatively automatic control could be used for the first part of the flight. Near the target area, the controller will select a target, guiding the missile onto it with a very high degree of precision. Such devices are perhaps more correctly placed in the category of guided missiles than rockets, but the long ranges of 10km (currently possible) and 25km or even 50km in the future make them competitors to both guns and rockets for the accurate engagement of high value depth targets.

ELECTRONIC WARHEADS

The requirement for NLW effects could encourage the development of new types of warheads for shells and rockets. Small electronic jammers have already been fitted into 152mm and 155mm shells by the Russians and the United States, and it is likely that smart versions of such warheads, which operate only when they sense a transmission, will follow.

FIREPOWER

Whatever other requirements are sought for future weapon systems, it is almost certain that they will include a need for greater firepower if only to justify the replacement of a current system. It can be argued that most of the preceding ideas contribute to improved firepower but there are at least two other developments of significance.

Automation

Firstly, improved automation especially in the handling of ammunition should improve rates of fire and it also has the benefit of reducing manpower around the weapon platform. Rocket systems such as the MLRS demonstrate this advantage, but automation has so far been adapted less readily to guns. The main problem is in reloading SP gun turret stocks from external supplies. The most obvious answer is to procure a specialist resupply vehicle, such as the US Army is doing with the Field Artillery Resupply Vehicle (FARV) for their next generation Crusader gun. This is armoured to improve detachment survivability and has a conveyor belt to feed the gun with shells from a position just to its rear. Propellant, fuel and food will also be resupplied, allowing the gun the ability to remain in action while only the FARV moves to resupply points. It is possible that Crusader and the FARV will each have a detachment of three men, the total of six being far less than the war establishment of twelve for typical current medium calibre guns such as the M109 and its supply vehicles. The penalties are the cost of the specialist vehicle and the time and effort spent in reloading it. For these reasons the British Army is pursuing an alternative approach of using small devices such as roller trackway to assist in ammunition handling between ammunition containers and guns.

Handling of ammunition inside an SP gun can also be a problem, especially if high rates of fire are required. Fully automatic loaders are the obvious answer and one of the most advanced is built into the French AUF-1 or GCT 155mm gun. The rear of the turret of this gun contains stacks of ammunition which can be externally reloaded fairly easily. Loading of both shell and charge are fully automatic. The autoloader takes up considerable space but of course the crew can be reduced. Evidently such a system must be highly reliable and it must be so arranged that manual operation is not too difficult and slow, in order to provide a reversionary mode.

Robotics

The logical extension of automation is to incorporate robotics into a gun or rocket launcher. This implies the use of more versatile mechanisms controlled by computers, and in time they might replace most or even all of the gun detachment. Such systems would need to have very high reliability levels since experience from civilian use suggests that they are unlikely to allow easy manual reversionary operation. The possibility can be envisaged of a battery of guns being controlled remotely by a small command post crew, but the cost and time needed to develop such equipment would make it a very long-term aim for the foreseeable future.

Thermal Management

A further factor which can limit firepower is barrel heating. This is often overlooked or at best accepted as a limitation. The high rates of fire of more than six rounds in one minute that are possible from modern guns will cause barrels to heat above safe temperatures if fired at high charge and if sustained for too long. The use of propellants with a high piezometric efficiency (i.e. low heat generation for a given pressure) can reduce the problem but cannot solve it. Obviously, warning of immediate charge cook-off would be an advantage, and this can be achieved relatively simply by inserting thermocouples into the barrel near the chamber. Rather more useful would be a prediction of when, given a projected firing timetable, a gun is expected to become too hot to fire or, better still, how the firing plan could be modified to avoid overheating. Current research to develop a computer program to do this appears promising.

Barrel Cooling

Ultimately, if barrel heating problems are not to become a serious limitation to the rate of fire, some means of artificially cooling the ordnance is required. Blowing air through the bore is possible but the specific heat of air is not high enough for it to absorb sufficient thermal energy from the barrel if firing is to continue at high rates. Research has shown that a liquid with a high specific heat is required. Spraying the bore with water has been tested but arrangements for doing this and removing any residue in between successive rounds are complex, and there is a danger that the direct cooling effect could alter the material properties of the barrel near the bore. The most promising solution appears to be to make the barrel with internal tubes through which a liquid is pumped. The liquid can be taken to a radiator where it is cooled before being recycled and the complete process is similar to cooling an engine. Constructing ordnance in this way would obviously be more expensive than standard solid walled barrels.

MOBILITY AND WEIGHT

The major mobility improbvement requirement for indirect fire weapon platforms is to produce a 155mm towed gun which can be carried by a medium support helicopter. This will a weapon with a good target effect (compared to 105mm shells) to be fired from a platform which can have good strategic and operational mobility. In order for a lightweight gun to absorb the firing stresses and remain stable, designers need to use both high-strength low-density materials such as titanium and aluminium alloys, and also somwhat unconventional designs. Such materials are used in the construction of two contenders for the US requirement for this type of system, and for the future British Lightweight Mobile Artillery Weapon System. The Royal Ordnance Lightweight Mobile Artillery Weapon System. The Royal Ordnance Lightweight Towed Howitzer (see Figure 7.7) also uses a 'curvilinear' recoil mechanism to increase artificially the weight of the howitzer during recoil.

Figure 7.7 The RO Lightweight Towed Howitzer (prototype)

The Vickers Shipbuilding Ultralightweight Field Howitzer (see Figure 7.8) has very low trunnions and its centre of gravity is well forward, all of which help to maintain stability.

Similar requirements are being demanded of rocket systems to make them more mobile. HIMARS is effectively a lightweight version of MLRS, capable of firing just one pod of six rockets rather than two pods. It is built on a wheeled truck chassis rather than on an armoured tracked chassis, which allows it to be carried inside a C130 Hercules aircraft for rapid strategic deployment. Once in the operational area its wheels will allow it to move faster along roads although its tactical mobility across country is likely to be inferior to the tracked MLRS.

New Materials

The use of high strength to weight materials has already been mentioned as a means of reducing launcher weight, although it must be realised that they are likely to remain expensive for the foreseeable future. The choice of material will depend very much on the nature of the loads to be applied to it. Metal alloys are likely to be required where both linear strains and bending moments are present, such as in the trails of a towed gun. However, carbon fibre might be suitable for the construction of composite barrels, steel being used for the

Figure 7.8 The VSEL Ultralightweight Field Howitzer (prototype)

inner section including the bore where it provides high wear resistance, and carbon fibre being wrapped around the outside where its high tensile strength can resist hoop stress.

CONCLUSION

This chapter has considered a wide variety of developments in the design of indirect fire systems. Many of them will appear in service equipment used by a variety of armies within the next ten years. Others are possible, but less likely, and no doubt some developments not mentioned here will appear before long. What seems certain is that unless there is a major conflict involving the few pre-eminent military nations, developments will only be brought to production and use by soldiers if they are seen to offer significant enhancements to military capability of the type suggested in the requirements section at the beginning of this chapter.

Glossary of terms

Abrasive Wear	See 'Wear'.
Accuracy	A measure of the precision with which the MPI of a group of rounds can be placed on the target.
ADP	Automatic Data Processing.
AFAS	Advanced Field Artillery System.
AFATDS	Army Field Artillery Target Direction System.
AFV	Armoured Fighting Vehicle.
All-burnt	The term used to describe the stage in the sequence of events when a gun is fired at which the propellant is completely consumed.
Angle of Sight	The vertical angle between the horizontal plane through the weapon and the line of sight to the target.
APC	Armoured Personnel Carrier.
Articulation	The method by which the four points of contact of a split trail carriage maintain contact with the ground when it is uneven.
ASTOR	Airborne Stand-off Radar.
ASTROS	Artillery Saturation Rocket System.
ATACMS	Army Tactical Missile System.
Autofrettage	A process of pre-stressing a barrel by stretching the inner layers of metal beyond their elastic limit but at the same time stretching the outer layers within their elastic limit. The effect is that the outer layers compress the inner layers. There are two approaches to this process: 'Hydraulic Autofrettage' and 'Swage Autofrettage'.
Autonomous Munition	A munition which contains a seeker and guidance mechanism allowing it to hit a small target without external targeting assistance.
Axis of the Bore	The straight line passing through the centre of the bore.

B

Balancing Gear	A device used to counteract the out-of-balance moment present when the trunnions are not located at the centre of gravity of the elevating mass. 'Equilibrator' is another term used for balancing gear.
Ballista	An ancient, mechanical, torsion-powered weapon for hurling missiles.
Ballistic Coefficient	A measure of a projectile's carrying power. It is a function of the projectile's mass, diameter, shape and coefficient of steadiness.
Ballistics	The study of the motion of projectiles.
Barrel Clamp	An arrangement to prevent damage to the elevating gear by preventing movement between the basic structure and the elevating mass when the gun is on the move. See also 'Cradle Clamp'.
Base Bleed	A technique for reducing Base Drag and hence increasing the range of a projectile by filling the partial vacuum behind the shell with gas from a generator in the base of the shell.
Basic Structure	That part of a gun in contact with the ground. It transmits the firing stresses to the ground and supports the 'superstructure'.
BAT	Brilliant Anti-Tank, a type of submunition developed for MLRS/ATACMS.
BATES	Battlefield Artillery Target Engagement System: the British Army's artillery ADP system.
Bedding-in	The process of fixing a mortar baseplate firmly into the ground by firing to ensure that it does not rock during subsequent firing.
BL	Breech Loading (see 'Obturation').
Bomblet	A warhead submunition usually designed with both shaped charge and fragmentation effects.
Bore	The interior of a barrel from the rear of the chamber to the muzzle.

Breech	A mechanism used to close the end of a gun when the projectile is loaded and to withstand the rearward pressure of propellant gases when the gun is fired. In QF equipments it supports and extracts the cartridge case. In BL equipments it provides the means of obturation. It also carries the firing mechanism.
Buffer	A cylinder containing oil, springs, gas or a combination of these for the purpose of controlling and arresting the recoiling parts during recoil.
Built-up Barrel	A type of barrel constructed by shrinking two or more concentric tubes in such a way that the inner tube/s is pre-stressed.
Burst Fire	A high rate of fire produced in a short period. For 155mm equipments a rate of three rounds in 15 seconds or less is usually described as a burst-fire rate.

C

C^4	Command, Control, Communications and Computation.
Calibre	The diameter of the bore excluding the depth of the lands.
Calibre Length	The bore length expressed in calibres.
Carriage	An equipment that fires with its wheels in contact with the ground.
Chamber	The smooth portion at the breech end of the ordnance shaped to accommodate the charge.
Commencement of Rifling	The point in the bore where the grooves reach maximum depth.
Compensating Sight	A sight that compensates for drift.
Composite Barrel	A barrel made of several inner tubes each of different steel strengths and thicknesses, normally surrounded by a single outer tube.
Consistency	The measure of the degree of spread of a group of rounds about their MPI. The smaller the spread the better the consistency.

143

Control to Run-out	The means or method of controlling the final stages of run-out to prevent the recoiling parts from jolting back into their original position before firing.
Convergent-Divergent Nozzle	The commonly used type of rocket nozzle employed to change heat and pressure energy into kinetic energy. Sometimes called a 'De Laval Nozzle'.
Cradle	The component of the superstructure that carries the ordnance and enables it to slide axially on recoil. It is pivoted about the saddle to allow the ordnance to be elevated and depressed.
Cradle Clamp	An arrangement to prevent damage to the elevating gear by preventing movement between the saddle and the elevating mass when the gun is on the move. See also 'Barrel Clamp'.
Cut-off Gear	A means of shortening length of recoil when the gun is elevated.

D

De Laval Nozzle	See 'Convergent-Divergent Nozzle'.
Depth of Rifling	The measurement of rifling depth in the bore of a gun taken from the top of a land to the bottom of the groove.
Dial Sight	An optical indirect fire sight used for applying a bearing to a gun.
Direct Fire	Fire in which the weapon is directed at the target using the direct vision link between the sight and the target.
Drag	Resistance to the motion of a projectile through the air caused by the region of low pressure behind the base of the projectile: sometimes called 'base drag'.
Drift	The lateral deviation of a projectile in flight resulting from the spin imparted to it by the rifling of a gun.
Driving Band	A band (usually soft metal) fitted around a projectile for the purpose of engaging in the rifling.
DROPS	Dismountable Rack Offloading and Pickup System.

E

Elastic Limit	The stress limit for elastic as opposed to plastic deformation of metals.
Electro-thermal Gun	A gun which uses electrical energy in the chamber. An Electro-thermal Chemical Gun uses electrical energy, normally in the form of plasma, to augment the energy from chemical propellant in the chamber.
Elevating Gear	The gear arrangement that controls movement in the vertical plane of the elevating mass about the trunnions.
Elevating Mass	All parts of the equipment which elevate. In most cases it includes the ordnance, the cradle and the recoil system.
Elevation	The vertical (acute) angle between the horizontal plane and the axis of the bore.
EM	Electromagnetic.
Equilibrator	See 'Balancing Gear'.
ERBS	Extended Range Bomblet Shell.
Erosive Scoring	The localised removal or scoring of metal from the bore surface caused by an imperfect seal of the driving band allowing high pressure gas to escape forward. It most frequently develops on the upper surface of the bore close to the commencement of firing.
Erosive Wear	See 'Wear'.
ET	Electro-Thermal.
ETC	Electro-Thermal Chemical.
Extraction	The removal of the cartridge case or the vent tube from the breech.
Extractors	Mechanical devices for removing cartridge cases from the breech. They may also serve to hold sliding block breech mechanisms in the open position.

F

FACE	Field Artillery Computing Equipment: the British artillery battery-level ballistic computer. Now being replaced by BATES.
FARV	Field Artillery Resupply Vehicle.
Fatigue	The radial propagation of cracks from the inner surface of the bore of a gun.
FFR	Free Flight Rockets.
Finning	The raised, grooved surface found on some barrels, especially mortar barrels, for the purpose of improving heat dissipation by increasing the external surface area of the barrel.
Fixation	The process of determining the coordinates of a weapon system, an observation post, or a target.
Firing Lock	That part of a firing mechanism that carries the striker.
Firing Mechanism	A device for initiating the ammunition primer.
Firing Post	A term used to describe a fixed firing pin fitted into the base of a mortar barrel.
Firing Table	See 'Range Table'.
FOFA	Follow-On Forces Attack.
FOGM	Fibre-optic guided missile.
Foundation Figure	The envelope of the axis of overturning in the horizontal plane, as applied to gun stability.
Free Recoil Efficiency	A measure of the percentage reduction in recoil energy resulting from the use of a muzzle brake. It allows for free recoil during gas action and is corrected for the mass of the muzzle brake. (See also 'Gross Efficiency' and 'Intrinsic Efficiency'.)
Fume Extractor	An attachment to the barrel of an SP gun which ensures that propellant fumes do not escape into the crew compartment when the breech is opened.

G

g	gram.
GAP	See 'Gun Aiming Point'.
Girder Stress	The stress produced by the bending of a barrel by virtue of its weight and length.
Gross Efficiency	A measure of the percentage reduction in recoil energy as a result of a muzzle brake being fitted. It does not take into account the mass of the muzzle brake (see also 'Free Recoil Efficiency' and 'Intrinsic Efficiency').
Gun	Originally this term was reserved for comparatively long-range equipments firing a relatively small shell, usually a fixed charge, at a high MV and at a low trajectory. Nowadays the term is often used as a generic term for both guns and howitzers, although in some cases the distinction is maintained and in other cases when the equipment meets the characteristics of a gun and a howitzer the term 'gun/howitzer' is adopted (see also 'Howitzer').
Gun-Mortar	A breech-loading mortar, normally turret-mounted on a self-propelled chassis, which can be fired in the low angle.
Gun Aiming Point	A reference point, real or artificial, used during the engagement of targets by indirect fire to ensure that the weapon is pointing in the right direction.
Gunner's Quadrant	An adjustable set-square with a spirit level bubble, used when laying a gun for elevation as an alternative to the elevation sight.

H

HE	High Explosive.
HEAT	High Explosive Anti-Tank, a type of chemical energy warhead common on guided missiles.
High Angle Fire	Fire delivered by indirect fire weapons at elevations above that at which the maximum range for the equipment is achieved. In general terms it is fire above elevations of 800mils.

HIMARS	High Mobility Artillery Rocket System.
Howitzer	A comparatively short-range equipment firing a relatively heavy projectile at a low muzzle velocity and using variable charges (see also 'Gun').
Hydraulic Autofrettage	A process for pre-stressing gun barrels by the application of high fluid pressure (see also 'Autofrettage' and 'Swage Autofrettage').

I

ICM	Improved Conventional Munition. Normally used to refer to a warhead containing submunitions (e.g. see 'Bomblets'), which can provide a greater target effect than a unitary HE warhead.
Indirect Fire	Fire delivered at a target without the use of a direct vision link between the weapon sight and the target.
Intensification	A method of providing an improved pressure seal from the obturator pad in a BL breech.
Intrinsic Efficiency	A measure of the percentage reduction in the recoil energy to be absorbed by the recoil system as a result of a muzzle brake being fitted and corrected for the effect of the mass of the muzzle brake (see also 'Free Recoil Efficiency' and 'Gross Efficiency').

J

JSTARS	Joint Surveillance and Target Attack System.
Jump	The angle between the axis of the gun when laid and the line of departure.

L

Lands	The raised portions between the grooves of the rifling in the bore.
LARS	Light Artillery Rocket System.
Laying	The process of adjusting the gun for line and elevation.
LBM	Lever Breech Mechanism.

Lead	The aim-off applied to the sights to allow for the lateral movement of the target during the time of flight in direct fire engagements.
Line	Direction or azimuth when used to describe the process of laying.
Line of Departure	The direction of motion of a projectile as it leaves the muzzle.
Lock	The part of the firing mechanism that carries the striker. Sometimes referred to as a firing lock.
Longitudinal Stress	Stress in a gun barrel resulting from the action of the driving band and the difference in gas pressure between the front and the rear of the driving band. It causes a localised stretching effect along the length of the barrel as the projectile moves through the bore.
Loose Barrel	A type of barrel construction that incorporates a jacket over the highly stressed parts of the barrel to provide additional support. The barrel can be removed for replacement, or for stripping in the case of pack equipments.
Loose Liner	An earlier version of the loose barrel concept, the difference being that the jacket extends along the length of the barrel.
Low Angle Fire	Fire delivered at elevations below that at which the maximum range for the equipment is achieved. In general terms it is fire below 800 mils.
LP	Liquid Propellant.
LTM	Laser Target Marker.

M

Magnus Effect	One of the components of the drift of projectiles that causes projectiles rotating with right-hand spin to drift to the left if the nose of the projectile is above the trajectory or to the right if it is below the trajectory. It is caused by the build-up of air pressure on one side of the projectile.
MCS	Modular Charge System.

Mean Point of Impact	The centre point of the spread of a group of rounds fired from a gun at the same line and elevation.
Metal-to-Metal Obturation	A method of obturation used in some BL systems in which an insert in a sliding block makes close contact with a metal ring or bush mounted in the chamber face of the barrel. The advantage of this method is that a sliding block mechanism can be used with a BL ordnance (see also 'Obturation' and 'Obturator').
Mil	A unit of angular measurement. One degree = 17.8 mils.
MLRS	Multiple Launch Rocket System.
Monoblock Barrel	A barrel constructed from a single ingot of metal.
MORAT	Mortar Anti-Tank.
Mortar	An indirect fire weapon which, in its conventional form, is muzzle loaded, has a smooth bore, transmits firing stresses directly to the ground and only fires in high angle. Unorthodox versions using rifled bores and/or breech loading do exist. Some mortars also have a low angle capability.
Mounting	An equipment that fires without its wheels in contact with the ground.
MOU	Memorandum of Understanding.
MPI	See 'Mean Point of Impact'.
Muzzle Brake	An attachment to the muzzle of a barrel for the purpose of reducing the rearward momentum of the recoiling parts by deflecting sideways some of the gases emerging from the bore after shot ejection.
Muzzle Preponderance	The term used to describe the unequal weight distribution of a barrel with rear trunnions in relation to its centre of gravity. Barrels with rear trunnions are sometimes said to be 'muzzle heavy' which is another term used to describe the same condition.
Muzzle Velocity	The velocity with which the projectile leaves the muzzle.
MV	Muzzle Velocity.

N

NLW Non-Lethal Weapons.

Non-Rigidity of Trajectory The term used to describe the fact that, with indirect fire, targets at the same horizontal range but at different elevations must be engaged with projectiles following different trajectories.

Nozzle A component in the base of a rocket that changes the heat and pressure energy of escaping propellant gases into kinetic energy. The gases are expanded in the nozzle to lower temperatures and pressures, reaching a very high velocity in the process. The rate of change of momentum of the gases provides the propulsion for the rocket.

O

Obturation The prevention of the escape of gases produced by the charge, forward around the shell or bomb and rearward through the breech. There are two approaches to obturation:

(a) QF Obturation – in which the cartridge case provides the means of obturation.

(b) BL Obturation – in which the means of obturation is provided by a resilient pad which seals the rear of the chamber.

Obturator A resilient pad which fits in a coned seating at the rear end of the chamber of BL systems. On firing the pad is compressed and expands to prevent the rearward escape of gases (see also 'Metal-to-Metal Obturation').

Open Jaw A type of breech ring which is slotted in the rear face to accept the block.

Ordnance The term used to describe the group of components or assemblies in a gun comprising the barrel and its attachments, the breech and the firing mechanism. It is also used as a general term to describe guns, howitzers and mortars.

Orientation The process of initially directing guns at the required bearing for the subsequent engagement of targets.

| Out of Balance Moment | The moment caused by the displacement of the centre of gravity of the elevating mass from the trunnions. Its magnitude varies with the weight of the elevating mass, the distance from the centre of gravity to the trunnions and the angle of elevation. |

P

Pad Obturator	See 'Obturator'.
PE_l	Probable Error Line.
PE_r	Probable Error Range.
Platforms	The main part of the basic structure of some mobile mountings to which are attached the stabilising girders and wheels.
Platonisation	A means of achieving a constant rate of burning over a specific range of pressures by the addition of lead salts to the propellant.
Primer	A component in the base of a cartridge case. It contains a cap for initiation and an ignition charge for the propellant. It functions either by percussion or electrical means.
Projectile	A missile fired from a piece of ordnance.
psi	Pounds per square inch.

Q

QF	Quick Firing (see 'Obturation').
Quadrant Elevation	The elevation at which a gun is laid to achieve the desired range under the prevailing conditions.
Quick Loading Gear	A mechanism for allowing the ordnance to move to an elevation which allows easier loading while the sights are being set simultaneously.

R

| Radial Stress | The stress acting outwards on the walls of the barrel produced by the gas pressure generated by the burning propellant in the bore. |

Range	The distance in metres between gun and target.
Range Table	A compilation of data on the performance of a gun produced at firing trials and used as the basis for the calculation of gun data for the engagement of targets. Sometimes called a 'Firing Table'.
RAP	Rocket Assisted Projectile.
Reciprocating Sight	A sight that allows for lack of level of trunnions.
Recoil	The rearward movement of the ordnance on firing, relative to the mounting or carriage.
Recoil Cycle	The term used to describe the rearward movement of the ordnance (recoil) and the return of the recoiling parts to their original position (run-out).
Recuperator	The component of the recoil mechanism that returns the recoiling parts to their run-out position and holds them there at all angles of elevation.
Regenerative Ignition	A self-controlled means of gradually igniting liquid propellant in the chamber of a gun.
Remaining Velocity	The velocity of the projectile at the point of impact.
Replenisher	A reservoir containing oil under pressure for maintaining an adequate volume of oil in the buffer of a recoil mechanism.
Rifling	The system of helical grooves cut into the bore for the purpose of imparting spin to the projectile.
Rocking Bar	A type of sight that enables an elevation to be set on the elevation scale, which in turn tilts the sight bracket through the same angle. Sight and ordnance are elevated together until the bubble on the sight bracket is level and the desired elevation is thus applied to the ordnance.
RPC	Rocket Pod Container.
RPV	Remotely Piloted Vehicle.
Run-out	The return of the recoiling parts, after recoil, to their original positions.

S

SADARM	Sense And Destroy Armour: a terminally guided sub-munition.
Saddle	The component of a gun's superstructure that carries the elevating mass but does not elevate with it. It traverses on the basic structure and is connected to it by some form of holding down arrangement.
Saddle Support	The part of the basic structure that supports the saddle. The trails and the wheels are attached to it.
Screw Breech	A type of breech mechanism that employs mating threaded surfaces on the breech ring and the breech block (screw). Sometimes called a breech screw mechanism.
SGI	Spheroidal graphite cast iron.
Shaped Charge	A type of warhead with its explosive charge shaped in such a way that the explosive energy is focused into a powerful and highly penetrating jet. The effect is sometimes called the hollow charge effect, the Newmann effect or the Monroe effect.
Shot Ejection	The point or moment in time at which the projectile leaves the bore.
Shot Seating	The conical portion of the bore where the chamber diameter is reduced to join the rifled portion.
Shot Start Pressure	The level of bore pressure at which the projectile begins to move.
Shot Travel	The distance along the bore between the base of the projectile (when loaded) and the muzzle.
Sight	The instrument used to direct ordnance in the required bearing and/or range.
Sliding Block	A type of breech mechanism mainly used in QF equipments but has been used for BL equipments. Its main components are the breech ring (either open or tied jaw) and a sliding block to close off the breech. The block can be designed to slide either vertically or horizontally.

Slipper	A gun component that connects the barrel to the cradle and the recoil system. It includes arrangements to prevent the barrel from turning and also takes the longitudinal thrust on firing.
Smart Munition	A munition containing a seeker and control mechanism which allows it to locate and guide itself onto a target.
Soft Recoil	A system of recoil that requires the recoiling parts to be held back under tension on a latch before firing. On firing the recoiling parts are released, before charge ignition, so that their forward momentum reduces the amount of recoil.
Sole Plate	Part of the basic structure of some mobile mountings. It provides a contact point with the ground and permits a limited top traverse.
SP	Self-propelled.
Spade	An attachment to the trail of a gun that prevents movement to the rear when the gun is fired.
Split Block Breech	A type of breech mechanism which combines the speed of action of a sliding block with BL obturation, thus avoiding the need for a cartridge case.
STA	Surveillance and Target Acquisition.
Stabilising Girder	The component of a mobile mounting that performs a similar function to the trail of a carriage.
Stability	Mountings and carriages are considered stable if the main supports remain stationary during the recoil cycle. A munition is considered stable if it does not tumble during flight.
Superstructure	The group of components of a gun above the basic structure, all of which traverse.
Swage Autofrettage	A method of autofrettage in which an oversize mandrel or swage is forced through the bore to overstrain the inner layers of metal. The advantage of this method is that it can be used to pre-stress barrels at pressures that are unattainable by hydraulic autofrettage (see 'Autofrettage').

T

Tangent Elevation	The vertical (acute) angle measured from the line of sight to the target and the axis of the bore.
TGSM	Terminally Guided Sub Munition.
Thrust Misalignment	A contributing factor to inaccuracy in rocket systems arising from any displacement between the axis of thrust and the centre of gravity of the rocket.
Tied Jaw	A type of breech ring used in sliding block mechanisms. The breech block recess is cut transversely through the ring, the rear face of the ring being cut away only sufficiently to enable loading. Inherently stronger than open jaw type but more difficult to manufacture.
Time of Flight	The time taken for the projectile to reach the target after the gun is fired.
Tip-off	The tendency of the nose of a rocket to tip downwards on leaving the launcher rail. It is prevented by launcher design that permits the simultaneous release of front and rear rocket holding points.
Torsional Stress	A twisting effect within the barrel wall caused by the rotation of the projectile as it proceeds up the bore.
Trails	The components of the basic structure of a carriage that transmit firing stresses to the ground, keep the weapon steady in the firing position and connect it to the prime mover.
Trajectory	The curve described by the centre of gravity of a projectile during its flight.
Traversing Gear	The gear that controls movement in the horizontal plane between the saddle and the saddle support.
Trough Cradle	A type of cradle, shaped like a trough, which houses the recoil mechanism.
Trunnion Pull	The force at the trunnions parallel to the axis of the bore, less the component of the mass of the recoiling parts.
Trunnions	The point about which a gun elevates.

156

Trunnion Tilt	The angle by which the trunnion axis deviates from the horizontal.
Twist of Rifling	The length of bore, expressed in calibres, in which the rifling helix describes one revolution. The twist can be either uniform or varying.

V

Vent Tube	The ammunition component used in BL charge systems to initiate the igniter bag attached to the propellant charge.

W

Wear	There are two main types of wear in barrels: 'erosive wear' which is the removal of metal from the bore surface by gas action, and 'abrasive wear' which is the removal of metal from the bore surface by mechanical friction between the projectile and the bore.
Welin Breech	A type of screw breech mechanism with interrupted threads on stepped segments. The threads are cut on varying radii to achieve a large bearing surface, although only a small turning movement is needed to screw the breech home.
Windage	The difference between the diameter of the bore of a mortar and the diameter of the bomb.
Wire Wound Barrel	A type of barrel construction in which pre-stressing is achieved by winding wire under tension on an inner tube.
WP	White Phosphorus.

Y

Yaw	The angle between the axis of the projectile and the tangent to the trajectory.

Z

Zero Length Launcher	A type of rocket launcher in which the first motion of the rocket removes it completely from the constraint of the launcher.

Bibliography

I.V. Hogg, *'A History of Artillery'*, Hamlyn, London (1974).

O.F.G. Hogg, *'Artillery: Its Origin, Heyday and Decline'*. Hurst, London (1970).

'Jane's Armour and Artillery', Jane's Publishing Co., London (1995).

'Jane's Defence Weekly', Jane's Publishing Co., London (various copies).

'Journal of the Royal Artillery', RA Institution, Woolwich, London (various copies).

Index